MW01482143

Praise for
The Nonprofit Book of Wisdom

Nonprofit CEOs and executive directors have never had it easy.

As Sheree Allison writes in *The Non-Profit Book of Wisdom*, executive directors are expected to "know every facet of business and execute at near-perfect levels…all while working for a committee of volunteer employers in the least optimal conditions with a shoestring staff at the lowest possible compensation."

It's easy to get exhausted in the nonprofit sector…*to forget what drew you in the first place.*

And now, in the middle of a global pandemic and worldwide uprisings, CEOs are pivoting so fast their heads are spinning. They're redefining their missions. They're figuring out how to increase their services…when funding has often decreased.

What nonprofit CEOs and executive directors need today is not more "how to." There's more than enough of that to go around. What EDs and CEOs need right now—and every day—is pure inspiration. Words of wisdom to propel them forward when the going gets tough. And it will get tough.

Nobody cuts through the absolute BS you will encounter quite like Sheree Allison. And in *The Nonprofit Book of Wisdom*, she draws on a powerful combination of time in the trenches and hard-won lessons to let you know that you are not alone. This book is easy to read and incredibly effective. Highly recommended for all nonprofit CEOs and executive directors (and it wouldn't hurt to get a copy for the board too).

— *Pamela Grow, fundrasing coach for small non profits*

Sheree has more than 30 years as a non-profit executive director and she has packed decades of wisdom in this book. It's a how-to-prosper, and a what-to-avoid resource guide for current executive directors. Or those who want to become an executive director. This is a much-needed gift in this time of rapid transition within the sector.

— *Harvey McKinnon, author, The Power of Giving*

Einstein famously said: *"Wisdom is not a product of schooling but a lifelong attempt to acquire it"*. Sheree Allison's journey bears witness to that.

Her book is indeed a Book of Wisdom, wisdom to be heeded by every executive director or CEO and board of directors of nonprofits. It should also be an eye-opener for those members of the public who, not understanding the magnitude and the complexity of the work of these organizations, are too often indifferent to or dismissive of the importance of their contribution.

Business owners and managers also, would benefit from taking a page out of Sheree's book. Doing so would help deepen their understanding of the value of their staff and their worth for their organization and, the importance of insuring that the leadership and staff relate to the numbers they need to deliver individually for the business to succeed as a whole.

Sheree Allison is the epitome of a strong and effective leader. Based on conventional wisdom, a strong leader must be tough. Not Sheree. What defines her as a leader is not being tough, it is being kind. However, she does not tolerate 'average' or 'good enough'. The standard she has always set for herself, and what she expects from others, is to do it right and do it the best, that is, keeping at it until you figure it out. This is how she took the non-profit that she led for over 30 years to a soaring level of success.

—*Aldéa Landry, President, Landal Inc.*

I loved this book. In fact I've already started quoting extracts.

You should read this book if you are the executive director of a non-profit, whether you are newly promoted or experienced but believe you can do better still. It's also insightful if you are thinking of entering the charity world and want an honest view of the foibles that make this sector unique and challenging.

From the opening, where Sheree describes possibly the worst first week on the job ever, this book tackles real problems with a positive tone and practical solutions. She acknowledges the truth about conflicts with board, and staff that don't cut it. She has seen problems you haven't yet—but you will! Sheree has been, as she puts it, on "the struggle bus", but survived and thrived by focusing on the mission not the mishaps.

She offers simple ways for you to be a good manager, from deciding who to hire to how to fire those employees who "dig their own grave". She also proposes the deceptively simple question you should ask your staff every morning (see page 34).

Sheree tells enlightening and amusing stories from her career, her ups and downs, in easy to read nuggets, in a breezy 175 pages. Each short section (perfect for reading in the bathroom?) ends with "Thriving Points" to give you food for thought.

You'll want to reread this book once a year (or more often) as issues confront you and you wonder *What Would Sheree Do?* You may not agree with every idea, but Sheree will get you thinking creatively.

— *Ken Wyman, Fundraising Consultant/Professor Emeritus*

A delightful mix of memoir and how-to, useful for new executive directors and great reminders for veterans.

Chock full of insight, stories and lessons from years of experience and reflection. This book will be helpful to EDS and anyone working with an ED.

An accessible and handy book about how to be a great executive director combined with fun stories and novel approaches to everything from staff recruitment to dealing with gossip. Useful for people new to their job, considering entering the nonprofit field, or simply wanting a reminder about why we do this work and how we can do it better.

— *Kim Klein, author, Fundraising for Social Change*

A delightful and inspiring read!

Unlike a "how to" piece, *The Nonprofit Book of Wisdom* by Sheree Allison is overflowing with the smarts, transparency, and grit that only someone with her passion, experience and record of success could conjure.

Yet it is vulnerable and caring — overflowing with stories of conquests and failures all woven with humour that keeps you smiling while totally engaged with the dialogue.

And, entertaining as it is, it's also chock-full of street-smart advice and tangible tools on running a non-profit successfully that beginning executive directors must learn and seasoned ones will ask, "Why didn't someone tell me this long ago?"

A must read for EDs, yes, **and** their boards.

—*Marcy Heim, The Artful Asker*

Sheree Allison's new book is full of thoughtful insights that can only be conveyed by someone who walks the talk!

Whether you're considering pursuing an ED role or you've already taken the plunge, this easy—yet important—read will be a lifesaver in the chilly and turbulent waters one can encounter at the helm.

Having known Sheree professionally for almost three decades I really appreciated her practical, knowledgeable, conversational tone. I could literally hear her voice in this text as her gentle wisdom unfolded before me.

I have enormous respect and admiration for all of you who consider, or have pursued the role of "chief executive" of a charity. Make no mistake, it's not for the faint at heart, but rest assured, this book is a worthy companion on this noble adventure!

—*Cynthia J. Armour, CFRE, Chief Executive/Board Trainer & Coach, Elderstone Resource Development*

When you find yourself in a leadership position with more questions than answers, charity sector veteran, Sheree Allison, provides a calm and reassuring reference guide to knowing what the right thing is, and how to go about doing it.

— *Gail Picco, Editor in Chief, The Charity Report*

Heartfelt insight from the lived experience of an executive director. Filled with pearls of wisdom translated into "thriving points" of learning. Written for not-for profits, yet relevant for anyone in leadership trying to manage mission, vision and values and live a "purpose driven life".

— *Leanne Fitch, Retired Chief of Police*

The Nonprofit Book
of
Wisdom

One Executive Director Who Couldn't Be Swayed

SHEREE ALLISON

 civil sector press

Nonprofit Book of Wisdom — One Executive Director Who Couldn't be Swayed

Copyright © 2020 Sheree Allison

All rights reserved. No part of this publication may be reproduced, stored in any material form (including photocopying or storing it in any medium by electronic means and whether or not transiently or incidentally to some other use of this publication) without the written permission of the copyright holder except in accordance with the provisions of the Copyright Act. Applications for the copyright holder's written permission to reproduce any part of this publication should be addressed to the publisher.

Warning: The doing of an unauthorized act in relation to a copyrighted work may result in both a civil claim for damages and criminal prosecution.

Library and Archives Canada Cataloguing in Publication

Title: The Nonprofit book of wisdom : one executive director who couldn't be swayed / by Sheree Allison.

Names: Allison, Sheree, 1960- author.

Identifiers: Canadiana (print) 20200298194 | Canadiana (ebook) 20200298917 | ISBN 9781927375556

(softcover) | ISBN 9781927375570 (HTML)

Subjects: LCSH: Allison, Sheree, 1960-—Anecdotes. | LCSH: Nonprofit organizations—Management. |

LCSH: Chief executive officers. | LCSH: Chief executive officers—Anecdotes.

Classification: LCC HD62.6 .A45 2020 | DDC 658.4/2—DC23

Nonprofit Book of Wisdom — One Executive Director Who Couldn't be Swayed

Publisher: Civil Sector Press
Canada
Box 86, Station C, Toronto, Ontario, M6J 3M7 Canada
Telephone: 416.267.1287
hilborn-charityenews.ca

United States of America
2626 Glenway Ave, Cincinnati, OH   45204 USA
Telephone: 513.471.6622

Editor: Jim Hilborn
Cover art: Anne Assaff
Book production: Cranberryink

This book is dedicated to Andrew Steeves, Allyson Steeves and Sam Bourque. May you always know what is actually important, real, and good.

"It is only in the heart that one can see rightly; what is essential is invisible to the eye."

—*The Little Prince,* Antoine de Saint-Exupéry

Vignettes

Introduction

I started my 30+ year executive director non profit career with absolutely no idea what I was getting into. Bright-eyed, bushy-tailed, and fresh out of leading a classroom full of eager middle schoolers — I waltzed into my first board meeting assuming we were all on the same team, we all had the same vision, and everybody loved me.

My wake-up call was fast and furious. Not only did I have to figure out the organization's rather brief history by reading only the minutes, three of the seven board members wouldn't even make eye contact with me. "That's odd. What's that all about?" I wondered. And of course, it was soon revealed.

If you're an executive director reading this right now, I know. I know where you are. I know where you've been. Above all, I know what you're up against. While I'm always optimistic and enthusiastic about fulfilling a nonprofit mission, I am simultaneously unromantic about what it takes to do that at the highest level of leadership.

It's always astounded me how few resources are available to those who pledge their lives to what is undoubtedly among the most thankless (unappreciated, unrewarded, overlooked, undervalued) roles a human being can take on. Executive directors are expected to know every facet of business and execute at near-perfect levels…all while working for a committee of volunteer employers in the least optimal conditions with a shoestring staff at the lowest possible compensation.

Inside this book, you will find a refreshingly powerful approach to the most critical concerns of every nonprofit. Whether you are eagerly entering the nonprofit world for the first time, or you've just exited a situation that left you with more questions than answers, I can promise you that mission fulfillment and personal success are possible for you.

Getting the most out of this book requires only one thing. You must *want*. Nearly every nonprofit leader I meet has one thing in common, which is that their "wanter" is broken. Cynicism and skepticism have taken over. If you are like most nonprofit leaders, you are no longer asking, "How can I?" Rather, you are simply stating, "I can't because…" You will find no solutions in this book from that viewpoint.

I am inviting you to give it another try. To *want* again. To *wonder* again. To *hope* again. To *believe* again. And above all, to *know* again. Only then will you be certain, if what you are reading, can serve you. And above all, serve the mission you've chosen to fulfill.

Sound Advice
for
Executive Directors

What brings people to work in the nonprofit sector?

—————————————•◦◦•—————————————

FIRST AND FOREMOST, IT'S AN AFFINITY FOR THE CAUSE. It can't be just a job, due to the many hats you have to wear. So whichever nonprofit it is, I'd say 90% arrive there because the cause had some trigger in their memory bank or their emotional psyche. It could be cancer. It could be heart and stroke. It could be museums…or orchestra. It's some love they've had maybe from long ago, and now there's an organization that does that. And that's exciting. That's the first draw.

But over the threshold, there awaits a whole gamut of demands, obstacles, and skills needed. Those things add up to a mountain. And the Mission, the call, or your love for the cause is like a tiny crumb on the floor, because everything else is so eyes-wide-open, overpowering, and overwhelming. A person arriving on the scene for the first time thinks, "Wow, I didn't know all this had to happen in the background. I didn't know that in order to have a food bank, we had to have logistics and gas and schedule the volunteers who put on an apron. And they have to be engaged and managed!"

All the complications of the real world are in the cause that spoke to you, and your trigger was, "I really like animals." Not only do you not know what's ahead of you, but also you don't know what has come behind you. So you show up all excited and motivated, and it's not a 24-piece puzzle for 4-year-olds. It's a 5,000-piece puzzle where all the colours are the same tone, and you have to figure it out. It takes attention and significant energy every day. You can't go in and put your head on the desk and think the clock will tick and the day will end. That's not how it goes in a nonprofit.

When you choose to enter the charity sector, you're in a fishbowl. Eyes are on you because you represent a cause, and you need the people in that surrounding area to support you with either time or money. In a fishbowl, everything gets commented on. Everyone can feel and see it. If you want to work where you're not noticed and you don't have to be accountable, go work in an ocean and drift along. That's easy to find and easy to do. But it doesn't work that way in a nonprofit, and that's really overwhelming for many people. The comment I've heard so often is, "We have to work so hard!" Yes, you do.

Layer that reality with a group of board members who are always themselves in flux and always struggling to understand their roles. And layer on top of that a CEO who is well-intentioned, but whose attitude, insights and vision will determine what goes on over that threshold. So you bump into an awful lot you didn't expect when you thought, "I really like that cause. My mom had Alzheimer's. I want to work for the Alzheimer Society." Then you step in and realize there's a database, liability insurance, money to raise, marketing to create and deliver, a Board, overhead, and standards. And it doesn't matter what size your shop is. All those elements are always there. It's massive.

Thriving Point:

Know and understand the magnitude of the career you've chosen. It's time you embraced it.

Who are you in the matter of the Mission of your organization?

THERE IS NOTHING MORE IMPORTANT than keeping the Mission of your organization front and center to the work you do on a daily basis. Set aside the money crisis for a minute. Set aside your hiring woes. Put your HR issues on the shelf for a while. What does your organization exist for? And why are you here?

I want to focus on the organization's Mission where I served as executive director and why organizations such as Big Brothers Big Sisters and Boys & Girls Clubs matter. But in fact, I'm speaking of any nonprofit that serves youth.

While I am not a parent, I am truly passionate about kids. Childhood is where you get your blueprint for the rest of your life. Between ages five and twelve, what you are exposed to and the people you meet plant the seeds for the rest of your life. What I hope for is that kids will hang on to the good things even if it—when it—gets dark. I wanted a role in that, and it was worth every minute.

Beyond that, parents need organizations like Big Brothers Big Sisters/Boys & Girls Club to fill in the gaps of what they're already trying to do. In so many cases today, parents are just trying to keep the roof over their head. It's a reality. It's easy to look at people who struggle and criticize, but show me something in life that isn't criticized. When a person is poor, they don't see opportunity. They don't see things that cost money because that barrier shut down in their mind a long time ago. It's easy to say, "They don't work," therefore they just "use the system."

But it's deeper than that. You have to look at their story, where they've been, and what changed in their world that brought them to where they are today. What we do in society is look at them and throw them away.

We had an eight-year-old girl in our building one day for the after-school program. We served snacks to our youth, including fruits and vegetables, but this little girl wouldn't eat our snack. She looked hungry and she was not in good health, but she never ate anything we offered her. She turned down everything she was offered. One day, a volunteer pulled out a turkey sandwich from her own cooler during snack time to eat herself. The little girl was looking at her, so she offered her half the sandwich. The girl immediately accepted it and gobbled it up. "They have turkey at the food bank," she said. As it turns out, most often you say no to new foods, or new ideas, because you base your choices on what you've learned.

The last ten days of the month are brutal for people who are poor. From the 20th on, there is no more money. We had a little girl tell us how happy she was about the breakfast program we offered at all the schools in our community. It was nearing the end of the month and she said, "There are five slices of bread left now, and I split them with my brothers and sisters." Not what you expected? Most people see poverty in a headline way. They don't feel it and they rarely experience it. This is the reality of a life of struggle and poverty for so many youth in our country and across the world.

The organization I served and the people in it are guardians for a Mission that sees to it that every child in the community who is marginalized in any way gets a chance. And if I had anything to say about it, they also got a new blueprint for life. Depending on the door of the youth organization you walk through, you will find the activity level and the level of engagement depends on the people involved. It's the strength of the people in the organization that will give strength to programs and fundraising, very much like any business. It's about who is there with the willingness to make sure it happens, and that it happens for the right reasons.

Do you feel the passion I had for the Mission of the organization I served as executive director? I promise if you walked in when I was there, you would've felt it there, too. Because that's who I was in the matter of it.

Thriving Point:

When it's all said and done, what matters is who you decide to be every day to fulfill the Mission of your organization.

Why didn't it work?

IT COULD BE A RECENT FUNDRAISING PROJECT. It could be a recent marketing effort. Or a new hire. Here's where people don't spend the time. No-one wants to look at why it didn't work. Instead, we look for something new, something more proven, something someone else did. You could be reflective and ask, "Well, why didn't it work?" And this question alone could be a game changer. But if you don't take the time to look, you'll never know. You'll go on to the next thing…likely some big new thing you think will succeed with little to no effort.

A dismal failure takes time before you can go back, poke around and do an autopsy. You're too emotionally attached to the failure, so you need some time and some sleeps. Few are wired to experience a big failure and then stand up, dust themselves off and say, "Why didn't it work?" So give it some time. Let it settle into you.

A routine failure, like a marketing campaign that didn't get the results, is much easier to look at and say, "Why didn't it work?" There were no major losses. It just didn't work. Did we know this? Did we know that? Had we considered X? All those questions are what you ask when things don't work. And it's the non-routine disasters that cause the greatest heartache.

For every fundraising project I ever did, we made a list of things that worked and didn't work. We did it in a group — usually four or five of us. All the key people were involved. We used a flip chart and markers, and we jotted down all the ideas that came up. Interestingly, people are often quick to give up. They don't really try things; they only *test* them. They roll it out and if it doesn't do well in round one, they automatically label it a loss instead of saying "Let's build on this." However, most things in life are incremental. Even in human relationships, you don't meet someone and say, "Let's spend the rest of our lives together." It's incremental.

The reason I started the "worked/didn't work" list is because when you go through a whole series of projects, let's say by seasons of the year or quarters of the year, by the time the next year rolls around, it's so easy to do it exactly as you remember, the same way you did it last time. However, if you have the "worked/didn't work" as the top page of your plan, it brings you right back to reality. The objective is to create a guide for next time.

With all the projects in the organization I served as executive director, we put our hands on the wheel for the long term. We didn't do one-offs, and we didn't do short term. If you looked at all the projects we had, they were all long term. That builds credibility and quality work.

"Why didn't it work?" is a question you want to lay over every project you do. When you report to the board, you want to share what didn't work. "Yes, we had success, and you saw those headlines. That's all true, but let's dig a little deeper. Here's what didn't work about it, and if we don't fix that, we aren't going to have that success next year." The board needs to know not only that you have insights on the happy stories and feel good, but also that you are listening and watching for what isn't working. Too many executive directors want to look good, sound good, and ignore the thorns...all the time. But not everything works.

Thriving Point:

Not everything works. Winning requires asking why it didn't.

Where is your Mission at budget time?

LET'S FACE IT. Dealing with the budget for the coming year makes you want to put your face on the desk... and that same intensity exists as you look at the current year-end results. You've got the reality of now. Chances are good that it's too late to make up for the shortfall. You're likely going to have a deficit. That's a tough pill to swallow as you look toward the new year knowing you need to put a budget in place.

There are two obvious monsters in the executive director's office at this time of year. The fundraiser and the board. The former must produce, and the latter must buy into the vision: this is what we want to raise money for; here are the programs we want to do; and here are the activities we foresee happening in the coming year.

If you're interested in transforming your organization's results in the coming year, it begins with zero-based budgeting. **Do not** take the budget you currently have, add incremental changes, and call it good. "Let's put this up 3%, this up 6%, this up 2%, etc." This is the road to nowhere, and it is among the top three reasons nonprofits stay on the struggle bus.

Start with a zero base. That will cause you to ask, "What programs and activities do we want to do for our Mission in the next year?" List them out. Then go to the numbers. Ask yourself, "What will it cost to have this?" This is what the Mission needs. Most nonprofits forgot long ago who they're doing the budget for. The only customer of the budget is the Mission. It is not the board. It is not the fundraiser. And it is not all the other masters you are dancing to right now.

Line item budgets invite nitpicking. How many times have you been in meetings and the board gets stuck on the line item for office supplies? Or the lease for the copier? Take the budget to a higher level. Start with programs. What is it that you want to do in the coming year? Yes, you need staff. Yes, there is rent. And don't forget cleaning. And those items feed into each program or activity of the Mission.

Cast the vision of what you want to achieve, break it down by programs and then allocate a portion of the line item (rent for example) to the program. Same for staffing costs. Decide how many staff you need to do the work, calculate the wage costs, and assign that cost to the program the person works in.

A program or activity of a nonprofit organization to meet its Mission, also incurs direct costs. Tie the costs in the budget directly to the program. It changes the conversation and forces the board to focus on the *why*. You can see why a board gets all tied up over a line-item budget. A standard list with dollars plugged into it doesn't give them context tied to the Mission.

This is a different way of thinking. Consider these two scenarios. You can say to someone, "This year, I'm going to raise $80,000 to plant an apple orchard." Or you can say, "This community has green space for us to develop an apple orchard. If we get a great crop in the first year, here's what we'll do with the apples. We'll take them to schools. We'll take them to the food bank. We'll do a community apple event." There's your Why. That is the vision of the apple orchard.

Once you've created the vision of the apple orchard,

you ask, "What would that cost?" And you start to list out all the cost centers to create the apple orchard. Maybe it's $80,000. First you anchored the need in the Mission. And now you have a picture of what it is, what it will cost, and why you should raise money for it. Or instead, you could, as so many do, keep things black and white on a ledger, with nothing to inspire and all kinds of unknowns that create fear. One works, and one doesn't.

Thriving Point:

Fear doesn't create a budget. Vision does.

Where do you find your best people?

How do you find the very best people for your organization? The answer is networking, but not networking the way you've heard of it or seen it. I know the standard definition of networking, and I never participated, because it has no value.

My network was built by watching people out in the world. I was always looking for where they could have a role in the organization I served as executive director. Everyone is a stranger first. What is their skill? What is their technique? What are they really good at? My approach to networking was unique in that I was looking for solutions, whereas most everyone else is looking for what they could get out of the relationship.

Awhile back, I talked with a woman who remarked that two of her houses had horrible basement problems, and she was having trouble finding someone who did basement work. I recommended someone I had never actually hired myself. It was someone I noticed several times as I drove by a particular property. Specifically, I noticed the quality of his equipment and how he kept his space tidy as he worked. This was three years earlier and I still had his card. I passed it on to her.

What I do is watch. I look for people who are doing their work with care, and I pay attention to everything. I listen to people whom I respect to discover who they're aligned with. If someone I know has a deep sense of doing things well, I hire the people they use. I don't want to do something over, and I definitely don't want to do something where there was no cost benefit.

When I see someone doing great work, I walk right up to them and tell them what they're doing well that has caught my attention. What I've learned is that if people look after the details in their work, the big parts of the project they're working on are also well-managed. I hand them my card and make them an offer, "Come talk to me and consider working for me in the organization where I work as executive director."

The response I get from people I approach is usually pleasant. They generally have one of three reactions. They're either happy someone has noticed their work, paranoid because they assume they're being stalked, or generally comfortable with the response, "I like what I'm doing now."

One thing I do differently than most: if I'm not going to do business again with someone, I let them know. If I don't let them know for whatever reason, I say nothing. It is not my role to diminish anyone else or any other business. I have the responsibility to deal, and if it doesn't fit my needs, I let them know. Degrading or diminishing achieves nothing.

My favourite people are strangers. Somewhere along the way, I discovered that we limit who we know by playing it safe. We hang with the same people and go to the same places, but some of the most profound moments I've experienced have come from a total stranger. We'll have this moment of exchange and I'll walk away and think — *wow!*

Everyone has a story, and who they are is maybe not who they present as right now, so I take the time to understand. I want to know as many people as possible, and that is precisely how I've built my network to be as strong as it is.

Thriving Point:

Your organization is built on connections, and your connections are built on strangers whose care and skill can transform your organization.

What is your staff worth to your organization?

MOST NONPROFITS see staff wages as a cost. Even worse, most pride themselves on their low wages. It's labeled "overhead" and boards fixate on preserving perception around the use of resources instead of doing what the Mission demands.

Executive directors who talk about staffing costs see it as a finite number. A line item in the budget, it's sitting there as a burden. They rarely look at the reality, which is that without staff, how does the Mission get met? It's great to have volunteers; they do important work. But how many businesses do you know that run only with volunteers? And can you *really* run a business with volunteers? People who come in for a little bit, do a little bit, and then move on?

Next time you're running around town, stop and look at a nonprofit that has an office front or storefront. Consider the person in that building who is executive director or manager. They've had experiences in life where they learned to do good work, but they most likely did not learn all of the ins and outs of human resources, marketing, board governance, programs, and all the hats that an executive director picks up when they get that job.

You *must* have staff. If they're doing really great work, and you're delivering on everything you say you'll deliver on, that's priceless. Then your job is to boldly rise above criticism and pay them a living wage plus. The plus is because you want to retain them. You don't want to cycle through people. You want to get great people and keep them. You get them and keep them by treating them respectfully for their compensation and their benefits. Don't give your staff a bandanna that says, "I work in a nonprofit; therefore I get paid low wages."

The message in the sector is often, "It's not about the money; it's about the meaningful work", and "Your heartbeats pay your bills." And so often, staff get hired and they're told, "Oh, there's no money for training," and "Sorry, there's no money for technology," and "Oh no, there's no money for conferences." And then staff are expected to use Windows 97.

No, that's not how it works. The willingness to accept a scarcity mindset is rampant. It's just incredible. I see it all the time.

One of the ways to make sure staff are compensated well and fairly is using salary scales. Every position including the custodian has a salary scale from Level 1 to Level 7. Every year, they move to a different level. The salary scale reflects years of service, a cost of living increase and whatever percentage increase is given. It is approved at the budget level during the creation of the annual budget.

Every staff position knows where they start and where they can go, and that is reviewed every year. Mainly, you want them to know that you treat them well and fairly. You also want them to understand there is progression, and where they will max out. It's not a detriment but a reality. Inside this model, all staff sign off on their salary scales. When they first start, they're told their starting wage, their anniversary date, and what they can expect to get paid at each level.

The other thing to do is give each staff person a

statement of benefits. What staff do not always see is the monetary value in what they get through a health plan, vacation time, statutory holidays, bereavement leave, professional development, and personal time. All those things are costs on top of their wage. If their salary is $40,000, it totals $52,000 when their statement of benefits is added. Is that cash in their pocket? No. But if a family member dies, they can leave for the funeral, which is a benefit for them and a cost for the organization. Staff are always surprised and grateful to be shown this. They never thought of it that way, which should not be surprising. Nobody teaches us what money is or what the true cost of things really is. And that is the root cause of scarcity.

Now monetary incentive is important, and it works for many. But what works for everyone is acknowledgment, recognition and saying "Thank you." Every Wednesday, we have a Gold Rush draw. There are seven people in that room and Cindy always looks after the ballot drum. One particular year, I knew it was her five-year anniversary milestone being employed in that project. Cindy has the enthusiasm of a teenager. She's reliable and great at her work.

Just before the Gold Rush draw, I said to all seven people in the room, "The most important thing we're going to do today is thank Cindy." I had a gift card for her from Sport Chek, because she loves sneakers, and a "thank you" card. I shared two or three things she does amazingly well, and how important she is to us, and she was beaming the whole time. She came into my office afterwards and said, "That was so amazing what you did." And I said, "Cindy, you are so worth it." That's the kind of thing that makes good people stay. They don't stay with *only* pats on the back, but recognizing good work goes a long way.

Thriving Point:

Constantly ask yourself, "What value is the staff producing and what is that worth?" Pay them accordingly, and remember the importance of acknowledgment, recognition, and saying "Thank you."

What is truly driving an executive director's compensation inside a nonprofit?

When a board is tasked with the responsibility of setting the compensation and benefits for its leader, consider how they do it. As humans, we do what we know.

Let's say three of nine board members come from government or the public service sector. They have a very predictable human resources infrastructure. If they serve a full career, they go out with a very predictable funded pension. It's very linear. Let's say another three of the nine board members are small business owners. They have their own shops, and they trade services or products for money. They aren't mega corporations, but they've been in business for a while. They support their own families on the feast-or-famine roller coaster that is self-employment. And let's say the final three of the nine board members are at or near retirement. They've had full careers doing various kinds of work. Two are perhaps still working, finishing up the last of careers that have spanned a good long time. Their kids are raised and they're preparing on some level for whatever is next in life for them.

This is what boards look like. It's that kind of cross-section of humans that gathers together, and that collection of people sits down to compensate their executive director. What I know is they're gonna go from what they know. And what I know for sure is what they don't know, which is the nonprofit sector. And that is an interesting challenge within nonprofits that nobody has dealt with or answered so far.

Imagine that a board gathers together to create an employment package for their executive director. Someone on the board suggests $52,000 per year in salary. The person who threw that on the table is a teacher. Her salary is in that neighbourhood and has been for some time. She's married and has a tenured position, and her retirement has been accumulating for some time. She thinks it's a fair number. So do two of the public sector government employees sitting across from her who each earn around $55,000 per year.

Here's the problem with determining compensation this way. There is a mega-difference between a teacher, who leads a classroom from a pre-set curriculum and is tasked with only one job along with some moving parts along the way, and an executive director of an organization tasked with five to seven different hats, including hiring, firing, financials and keeping the money flowing in, all the while staying focused on a singular Mission. How does $52,000 begin to compensate a person for that level of responsibility?

The board compensates its leader based on whatever philosophy they have in their heads individually. But this begs the question: Is that why we have the myth in society that nonprofit charity sector workers should be poorly paid? Or is it not simply because the people making that decision have no point of reference other than their own life experiences? No wonder the board meeting to review the executive director's compensation and benefits is typically put off, shoved aside, and ignored entirely. I wouldn't be excited about making that decision either if I was on a board.

Thriving Point:

Moving beyond the stigmas and sacred cows that exist in the nonprofit sector requires asking bigger questions and examining what historically has never made sense. You can either begin to question it, or you can continue being ruled by it.

How do you create connections that matter within your organization?

IT'S THE ROLE OF THE EXECUTIVE DIRECTOR to pay attention to the people you have on the inside, and the most logical place to begin is with the board. Your job is to look for opportunities to shift how people relate. Most of us are creatures of comfort. We sit in the same place. We talk to people we already know. We just do what humans do everywhere. But in the boardroom, it's important to mix that up.

When board members don't really know each other, you don't hear from your best people. People go quiet. They feel as if they don't belong and are not adding value. They see others as having more authority or knowledge. They feel that others have been there longer, so they "get it" more quickly. And they start having conversations in their head. And some think, "I really don't have time for this. I'm too busy. I'm trying to balance home and other things. I've got someone in my family who is sick. I've got my work." And they quickly put their hand on the door and start to leave because while they're with the group, they never really attach. All those observations that may not be true have convinced them, "Gee, I think I'll move off this board now."

We all do that. We join, we look around, and we think, "I'm not sure I fit here." You judge yourself by watching others. And if you get in at the ground floor and don't feel it's meaningful, you start to recoil and slip towards the door at every meeting. So as executive director, you'll find people exiting, resigning, and they'll always give you the "correct" reason. The real reason, however, is underneath. And we don't get it. We just think, "Okay. Well, we've got to get a new board member," and begin that pursuit instead of saying, "What could we have done to retain that person?"

It's not very different from being in your teens and going to a high school dance. You want to go and you're excited. You get there, and you have that moment of thinking "Oh no," because there's the cool group and the in-group and whatever else. You have to find your place. And many teens never find their place, and they never go back because they just didn't know how to handle or cope with what it's like to be there, and not belong.

In this particular context, we had a board dinner recently. The genesis of my strategy for this particular event was that I found myself walking out of events thinking, "I talked with only seven out of 18 people" or "I didn't get to speak with Maureen or Phil." It wasn't about the five or six I talked with; it was that I just felt I was incomplete and missed out on something. And it turned out the board chair felt the same way. The event wasn't well-rounded or complete because of the interactions we missed out on.

So going later into a three-course board dinner, I thought, "How can I ensure that everyone gets an opportunity around a table to talk to the whole room?" I had three tables of five people each and used place cards. The event was board member plus one. Some of them were totally new to the room, not even familiar from a board sense. Everyone had a place card, and I purposely separated the people who came to the dinner together. My strategy began by creating discomfort for everyone: the idea of doing something different is fueled with discomfort, and people don't like that. I started off with assigned seating, randomly placing people at the tables. Right before the second course, everyone moved according to the instructions underneath their plate at the table where they were sitting. And I did the same thing again with the final course.

The first time everyone moved, that discomfort was still there. However, by the second time everyone moved, they started to say, "This is really great." By the time the dinner closed, everyone was feeling energized. It stimulated people to have conversations they wouldn't have had because they usually sat where they were comfortable. As everyone left the dinner, what they couldn't stop talking about was the people they had conversations with whom they had never talked to before. They were excited about the time they spent with people they ordinarily wouldn't have.

Along the way in your career, you may well consider joining a board or be invited to join one. And you'll have some of those same feelings as when you went to that first high school dance. You'll feel like the odd person out because it's way out of what you know and do well. And many times the people in the room will be welcoming, but they don't get you quickly to a place where you think, "I add value, I want to be with people like this, and this is right for me."

That is the job of the executive director — to read the room. Ask yourself, "How can these people get to know each other in a different way than just coming in and sitting around the boardroom table?" Everyone sits on the same side in the same area with the same people all the time. You can go around and name where people are going to sit even before they sit down. You have to be finding opportunities to shift that. The people you're working with need time to do more than just get to know each other. It's also to get to understand how they think and what's important to them.

Thriving Point:

As executive director, a critical part of your role is facilitating meaningful connections among those who serve the Mission. It's how you remind them who they are and empower them to do their best work on behalf of the organization.

How do you work with your board chair?

WHEN YOU HAVE AN HOUR to cover the critical things with your board chair, you have to remember they landed in there like a parachute. They came from their world where there is both the personal side and the professional side. They aren't involved in the day-to-day business of the organization.

Upon my arrival at a meeting with the board chair, the first thing I did was recalibrate their brain regarding what it is we do here. The easiest way is to share something significant that just happened. Something that turns the Mission on in their brain. It could be a recent win, a success story, anything where I can say ABC happened and this is what it did. I let that settle for a minute. The Mission falls to the back when you're dealing with governance things, board things, strategy things, and budget things. They're not exactly the kinds of things that make the board chair say, "Gee, I want to parachute in there and spend an hour of my day." I knew I was bringing them all the same kinds of challenges that exist in whatever life they exited in order to meet with me. I'm mindful that being a board chair isn't easy.

At the same time, I was also aware that it doesn't work to walk into a meeting with the board chair and unload all my problems. It's certainly human nature to want to do that, and here's how executive directors so easily fall into that trap. You have an annual meeting and you get a new board. You have a new board chair who has never served as board chair before. Let's call him Bill. After that annual meeting, Bill is given the gavel. It's up to the executive director to work with Bill so he knows what he's doing, and that he's doing things that are board-related.

So the meetings go on between the executive director and board chair Bill for several months. They're meeting every two weeks for an hour. In month eight, there's a crisis burning inside the organization. The executive director is at the edge and overwhelmed…and it's time to meet with Bill on board issues. The first thing to land on the table between them will predictably be the crisis that's burning. And that's where things start to unravel. It comes from the cycle of frequency of contact and trust. It becomes so easy to discuss issues that are not properly board matters. Instead they are operational, and this is how the board chair gets their hands in it.

An executive director has to remember who they are when they're in a meeting with the board chair. That's the daily vitamin, because frequency and confidence will blind you. It will cause you to go to the board chair to get things figured out. That's when it gets messy. And that's when you begin losing your authority.

This is a very delicate relationship. The board chair is a direct liaison between the board and the executive director. They have to be informed, and they have to be thinking of the whole organization. Most of that information is provided to them by the executive director, and the two must work well together. Unfortunately, most of the time the board chair doesn't know what their role is. Mostly they want to pick up the hammer and use it. Board chairs tend to be solely the lead in whatever they do for a living. They are often the final decision-maker, so they're used to picking up the hammer and using it when they want to.

Inside your organization, however, the board chair is only one of the members of an entire board. As executive director, you are *not* the board chair's employee; you report directly to the *whole* board. To have a balanced, open, trusting relationship with the board chair, you must learn the dance early—right after the AGM. Until the next AGM, the board chair is the person with whom you will consult, debate, and co-create the team inside the boardroom.

Frequency and focus are two critical steps in that dance. Not too often, but frequently enough to keep informed on the key issues. That's how often you meet with the board chair. Bi-weekly is a good option. Keep the meetings focused on governance issues and the future. Ask questions. You will learn a lot from the board chair. Just stop talking. You have a lot to pour into them, and they have a whole different perspective that you can learn from and leverage for the good of the organization.

Always remember that no one likes surprises, especially the board chair. Your role is to keep the pipeline of information relevant, timely and succinct. Seek a spirit of trust and both of you will soon know the dance of when to lead and when to follow.

Thriving Point:

As an executive director, you must understand your role, the role of the board chair, and the dance between the two of you.

How do you take your nonprofit to a soaring level of success?

IF AVERAGE IS WHAT YOU PREFER to get up in the morning and do, I recommend you re-think working in the nonprofit sector. Moreover, I recommend walking away from it entirely. This has never been an issue for me personally, because all I've ever known is that I wanted to do the *best* job. I could be sorting marbles, and I'd want to do the best job right out of the gate. I could be putting cutlery in a drawer, and I'd want to do it right and do it the best. Good enough has never been how I approach anything.

Please understand I'm not talking about *being* the best. I'm talking about **doing** the best. There's a big difference. *Being* the best often means being competitive, driven and single-minded. And it's admirable for those who want that path. **Doing** the best means keeping at it until you figure it out, something I have always done. And doing the best work you can often shows itself in unusual ways.

A woman showed up at the organization where I was executive director. It was her first time in, and she asked to meet with me. We walked to my office, and she said, "What agency does your marketing?" I found myself trying to translate the question, because I thought, "What is an agency?" I responded, "Do you mean who does all our marketing?" She said, "Yes. I've watched it and wondered, is it one out of Halifax?" I said, "No, I look after the marketing. I guide it. I don't necessarily do it all, but I come up with many of the ideas."

She was beyond surprised. "Are you serious?" I

responded, "I've learned marketing from necessity. I've never studied marketing. I only have two skills: I listen and I watch. I don't know how to do things great, but I know when things don't work. So I guess I'm the agency you wondered about." She laughed.

Besides doing the best work you can, I recommend either developing or cultivating two attributes that have served me as long as I can remember. Those two attributes are patience and kindness.

If you asked a random person who deals with me, "What is she like?" "Kind" would come up fairly early on as one of the top words. It doesn't show up in a PR way like, "look at the great deed she did." I'm referring to gentle kindness. Some people call it being thoughtful. Others call it being respectful. I call it being kind, and that is with me from the time I awaken to the time I retire at the end of the day.

If I were out with somebody and I dropped them off, I wouldn't pull away until they got in their door, or drive off until they were in their car and driving away. Is that a huge thing? No. It's being thoughtful about the person you're leaving. Kindness is not something you work at; it's something you live.

What I know is that I would never have done very well in a workplace, a business, or an organization where average and mundane is okay. I am not interested in being a cog in the wheel, and as long as the wheel turns once in a while, everyone is happy and out they go. I needed to be creating and leading. I needed to be inspiring others to do their best work, and I needed to be doing those things every day or I wouldn't survive. Where do you stand on this matter in your own organization? It's a question worth asking.

The organization I led had great success precisely because I poured 100% of myself into it. It also allowed me huge latitude to do some really creative work, and to practice and hone my skills in marketing, fundraising, leadership, and human resources. I have all kinds of skill-sets I was able to practice and develop by default rather than by choice or by having qualified for the job. There's an energy and excitement that comes from that, and a sense of a job well done. Money isn't the motivator or the driver in a nonprofit. It's the memories, experiences and impact that make you think, "I couldn't buy that."

Thriving Point:

To reach a level of success you've not yet seen or experienced, develop or cultivate these three attributes in your nonprofit work. Do the best job you possibly can. Practice patience. And above all things, practice kindness.

How do you start your day as an executive director?

I BEGAN EVERY DAY by asking my staff a question. It's not an emotional question, but it's interesting what I got for an answer when I asked. It truly was *my* question; I claimed it. I'm not even sure the people with whom I used it knew how consistently I asked it. It was as common to come from me as the usual "How are you"?

When I arrived at the office in the morning and saw Nicole, I still had a jacket on. I'd not made my way to my office yet. And I would go to where Nicole was and issue a friendly greeting, and then ask, "What do you need from me?" Somehow that question triggered the person who heard it, because they tended to put right in front of me what was in their head, what might be driving them crazy, whatever terrified them, or whatever was on their mind in that moment.

There was a freedom they got when I asked that question. It triggered brutal honesty. Rarely did I ever get, "Oh nothing; I'm fine." I would go down the hall and ask the same question to everyone, and they would lay out for me the most pressing thing going on in their world. Something they needed someone to hear about.

As executive director I was there to lead, nurture, champion, and nudge my staff. Everything was made possible by the people who showed up in our building every day and dedicated themselves to doing the work of supporting the youth of our community. It's not something I could have ever done alone, and I never forgot that. So my jaunt through the building in the morning was part of how I helped my staff unload whatever was on their mind, freeing themselves to get on with the business of serving our Mission.

Thriving Point:

As an executive director, consider a question you can pose at the start of your workday that triggers momentum and movement in your staff.

How do you relate to the numbers in your organization?

YOU ARE DRAWN TO A CAUSE because you were moved to believe and take action on it, and you wanted to be involved. You've likely been touched by the cause or have been moved by the work, and it sticks with you. In nonprofit organizations, all the conversations and the stories are about inspiring someone…like getting them to do more and give more. At some point, you have to balance those actions with the reality of the numbers.

Many projects and campaigns are repeated over and over simply because no-one takes the time and effort to crunch the numbers. Instead, everyone remembers what a good time it was, and how much everyone enjoyed participating. And of course, it'll be even better next year! If you're like most nonprofits, you gloss over the sad reality that very often, it's not working. And the measurement of whether it's working or not is in the numbers.

But most nonprofits don't connect the dots. They settle for a lesser result and convince themselves the lower number is "not bad, pretty good, and we'll do better next time." There's a treadmill in nonprofits of avoiding numbers and doing it for other reasons — loyalty, memories, nostalgia and feelings. Repetition kicks in and failure continues to mount. When you set a target, are you putting your flag down and declaring "We *are* going to do this"? Or is it pie in the sky, "We *want* to raise this much," and the connection between the declaration and the result isn't there.

The numbers have no meaning if you don't know

how they got there or what they mean. Without that understanding and a conversation about their validity and implication, the program doesn't make sense. Its impact on your Mission can't be measured.

Nonprofits tend to think their work is different from that of the private or corporate sector. "Those businesses don't have heart. We have heart. We have a Mission, and we can't view it through the same lens as a for-profit business." But at the end of the day, you *have* to, or you'll struggle and fall behind. It's a root problem in the sector, and the real reason why entrepreneurial folk who join boards quickly become frustrated with the widespread lack of attention to numbers.

When nonprofits do pay attention to numbers, they're too often doing it for an external funder who layers an expectation on them. Fill out this form and this form and this form. But they don't really *own* the numbers they write down. They're doing it for someone else to get that crucial next grant. Unfortunately, however, that won't work; it has to be an *internal* numbers game. Staff and the leadership in the organization have to live the numbers every week if they're going to be successful.

When it comes to charitable giving, most of the money is given in the last three days of the calendar year. The biggest day for donations coming in? December 31st. Over 30% of the money comes in during December. Yet you could pick up the phone and call ten random charities on those three big days, and probably get voice-mail, because they're closed. What's happening at the organization on those three biggest days when people give money? For too many, the lights are out, the doors are locked, and everyone is getting ready to celebrate a new year. And that's why the numbers don't add up.

Every staff member who works in an organization must know their numbers.

Administrative Staff: This person's numbers do not include balance sheets and targets. Instead, they include things like how many times the phone rings before being answered. The question isn't who's going to get the phone. The behaviour should be how quickly can we answer it? And what's the turnaround for saying "Thank you" when a donation is received? Those are *real* numbers.

Custodial Staff: This person's numbers are inventory. There is no such thing as an unending shelf or endless supply. There's a quantity because there's a cost. You have three mops? Great, you should have three mops next week as well, because if you don't know what your stock is, you're not managing the resources of the organization.

Marketing Staff: One of the things the organization typically does is put out a calendar. Let's say it's 3,000 printed copies. These folk might see their job as design, content and production. But the true job is to make sure that when those calendars are printed (correctly, on time, and within budget), there's a plan to get them on the walls of people who support you. Don't tell me you printed 3,000 calendars. Tell me what you did with them and how they move the Mission forward.

Program Staff: How many visits did you make this month? How many volunteers did you recruit? How many dinners did you serve? How many shelter beds were used last night? You have to be able to speak to those numbers.

Executive directors: You have a bucket-load of numbers. You need to live them; and your job is to translate the numbers for everyone. When you talk numbers, you talk outcomes, and that's what inspires your staff, your board and the community. Heart-warming, memorable stories stick. Make sure you lace them with specific numbers of proof and promise.

It becomes a more efficient, reliable and effective organization when people know why they do what they do, what they have really achieved in terms of their Mission, and how they can talk about it. Every staff must have a bucket of numbers they are responsible for, and they need to understand what those numbers are and why they are important, because it's not all about money. The numbers are owned by the staff and board. Check the behaviours in your organization and you will see how the numbers are impacted.

Thriving Point:

Being drawn to a Mission also means being drawn to the numbers. Numbers gauge how effectively the Mission is actually being fulfilled.

How do you produce extraordinary results in the nonprofit world?

—————————— ⌇⌇⌇ ——————————

IT'S SIMPLE. It's behaviour you demonstrate yourself, and it's behaviour you cultivate in your nonprofit staff…You lead. You decide. You toss in your ideas. You ask questions. In short, you don't wait for permission.

Everywhere you look, people are waiting for permission. Waiting to be told everything to do. Waiting for a prompt to do something other than breathe. I suspect the screens in our lives have glazed us over. Not only do people not react to things; they don't solve anything. This is a real problem. People choose not to think, and it frustrates the hell out of me.

When I was executive director, the following scenario happened when I had a staff person come to me…

> Staff: "I need to meet with the principal of this school to get this program running." (The program started in mid-September.) "I reached out and the principal is away until late September, so I guess we aren't doing the program."

> Me: "So…what if the principal never comes back?" (The answer she wanted to give was that we probably wouldn't do the program.) "What is the purpose of reaching out to the principal? Do you remember?"

> Staff: "To get buy-in."

> Me: "Okay. So do you think there could be a someone else, maybe the vice or admin, who can give that to you instead?"

I had to walk her all the way through this. And even though I ran into it daily, it still blew my mind. So many human beings simply haul themselves onto a park bench and sit there and wait forever. When I come upon someone who is motivated and engaged, I'm wowed. It's so refreshing because it's not common.

I remember having quite a few new staff, and many who were okay with, "Oh gee, she's gonna be away so I'll just wait." They were young people who got a ribbon and passed. No winners or losers. They got the certificate anyway.

We had this little girl named Mary, and she had a Big Sister in her life from our organization. Kindergarten has a graduation ceremony. So Mary graduated from kindergarten, and her Big Sister went to see her the day after her graduation and brought her a gift. When Mary opened it but didn't seem excited, her Big Sister asked, "Mary, do you like your gift?" Mary said yes. Her Big Sister said, "You don't seem happy or excited." Mary responded, "I graduated from kindergarten yesterday, and today I'm at the same desk in the same class with the same teacher." It occurred to me that no-one told Mary what graduation is. She thought it meant going on to something else, graduating to something new.

There is a reality, which is that kids in this day and age have everything done for them. They don't have to earn it. Nothing is explained to them; they're just given everything. Then they grow up into the workplace, and when somebody tells them "no" they settle. Instead of rising up to the obstacle, they sit down. I'm hopeful for the one who at least says, "Hey, I hit a wall. What should I do?" Most are too accepting of other people putting obstacles in their way, and that's why they can't do it.

They don't own the result.

Executive directors in particular love to hide behind permission so they don't have to stick their neck out and make a decision. And too many executive directors love to keep their hands clean by doing the soft work.

Thriving Point:

To produce extraordinary results in your organization stand up, lead, and *own* the result.

What drives hiring in your organization?

THE TOP TRAIT I LOOK FOR when I hire is energy level. I watch them walk across the parking lot to the door. How a person walks tells me a whole lot. I'm not talking about mobility problems. I'm talking about zest, interest, focus and care. If they approach the door and the lobby with interest, I can see it. I can also see when someone approaches the door as if they were walking on a beach without a care in the world. If they walk in that way, we're going to have a conversation about that. My question will be, "What's on your mind?" Start with what you see.

If a person came for an interview and parked by the door, that sent a strong message. There is more than you in the world, and you just told me you think you're number one. In a nonprofit, close and convenient don't win the game. I watched how a person greeted others upon arrival. I watched how they handled themselves once they were in a new space for the first time for something they wanted, which is a job. Show me you want it.

If you spend lots of time on that first intake, you will often see the behaviour that tells you what is going to play out thousands of times in the workplace. It just gets amplified when they come to work. If you're lucky enough to see the crack in the foundation at intake, just know that crack is going to get wider, deeper, and longer unless you fix it. And sometimes, you just can't fix it. If focus or decision-making is a problem, and that surfaces when you meet them or interview them, accept that you're not going to be able to fix everything. Ask yourself, "How much time, money and energy am I going to spend trying to fix something that doesn't want to be changed?"

Of course sometimes you're going to get it wrong. You can run them through all the filters, use all your tools, and use your best judgment, but because you're human, you will get it wrong. Many times, looking back I said, "That is not the person I hired." It's a constant and complex piece of work to hire people, bring them in, and know what you're getting.

About every seven hires, I had a blip where it was not the best match. It's true that sometimes urgency made me shortcut the filtering and decision-making. There were times I had to have a hire in place in two weeks, and I didn't make the right choice. The important difference, however, is how you deal with it. You either deal with it quickly when you get it wrong, or you choose to suffer and do poor work. It's a triangle with three points. What language are you using to avoid it? What is the consequence of not acting? And how are you trying to make them feel?

Something to acknowledge is that people are not seeking jobs for life. They are seeking jobs for now, and nobody wants a job for life. No-one is thinking beyond now. The job market suffers from indecision just like everything else. It shows up in a candidate when you ask them what they're looking for in a job, and they don't know. You ask them what they're really good at, and you get mostly silence.

People play to their weaknesses, and that list of weaknesses came from somebody who pointed it out to them. And so often when an offer is made, they can't decide. The time from when a job is offered to yes is not always immediate. They're unsure because to say yes takes commitment. Indecision — reluctance to commit — is rampant in the hiring process, but it's not always an indicator of a good or bad hire, because indecision is part of our culture.

Thriving Point:

When hiring, let your first impressions tell you what to build on and what you have to fix.

How do you approach obstacles in your work?

THINK ABOUT HOW you walk into your work each day. Do you just dive in, or do you ask lots of questions first? Do you see mostly possibilities…or obstacles? You can be certain that the way in which you approach your work has a big impact on your results. And it's more than you realize.

I've never been a mental gymnast. I just jump in. A great example was my very first day as an executive director. Mike was the board chair of the organization at the time, and I met him at his office. He suggested I leave my car, and off we went to a destination unknown to me. On the way, we stopped at a hardware store. He purchased paint, a paint roller and a pan. We left and arrived at what was introduced to me as the office. What I didn't notice was that the paint, paint roller and pan came into the office with us, too. Mike said, "This is your office. We just rented it. This is our new space, and you'll want to spend your first day getting it painted." It was a storefront in an older business, about 500 square feet with a single-use washroom. There was a desk, a chair, and a phone. The front door led onto the street.

Looking back, I see that it was wise to have something tangible to do that first day. Mike left and said he'd be back at 4 p.m. I had nothing to open the paint can with. He hadn't thought of that. So I went next door to borrow a knife. If you've never painted before, you get a lot on your hands. It wasn't water-soluble. And I definitely didn't dress for the occasion.

I did have a moment thinking, "I wonder what I'm doing tomorrow." The difference between the first and second day was that Mike didn't show up with a can of paint. Instead, I showed up alone with a key. I could either do some really great stuff or sit and look at the walls I had painted the day before. This is the epitome of my "just do it" motto. It's how I created true success in the organization where I served as executive director for over 30 years. I moved through all the little obstacles. You can either sit down and watch paint dry, or you can push through and get it done. And my initiation didn't end there.

I was hired by a small committee in June: three people around a little table. I wasn't told there was a board. In my mind, a board was something you put a nail into with a hammer. Mike wasn't part of the three who hired me, and I didn't understand that there was a larger complement of people who sit at a larger table called a board.

On my second day, another board member dropped by and gave me a box. In it was a binder that included minutes and reports of things that had gone on previously. It was an accounting of what had happened up until that time. It had no context, but as I started reading through it, I did get flavour.

In the 100 days before I arrived, it was the flavour of people who were fighting and quitting. People weren't happy that the other executive director was no longer there. The board chair had left, and the reason we had a new office was because the old office was in the building she occupied. So then I understood why I was new, and why we had a new space. That gave me a little bit of context, but not around the right issues. I just knew people were unhappy.

I also got a visit from someone whose name I don't remember. They said, "The old office used to be over there, and there are some things you'll have to go and get." What I didn't put together in the moment was that I had to go face Helen, the former executive director who had exited. It was a rainy Wednesday at 1:00 p.m., and I called her ahead to say I was coming by.

I walked up 14 slippery stone steps. When Helen opened the door, she threw a box at me like it was a basketball. I caught it, and I suddenly slipped and fell down the stone steps and broke my ankle. Shaken, I drove myself back to the office, walked on my ankle the rest of the day and the next, and did not go get it treated until Friday, obviously a mistake. Sometimes I think back to Helen and the fact that she closed the door in my face as I tumbled down those concrete steps. That's the depth of the angst of the organization when I joined. That day I was just a person showing up to pick up a box of remnants. I remember getting in my car thinking, "I know why they got rid of her."

It was a horrible experience, and I've only told this story to perhaps three people in my life. I thought, "I'm not going to make this street-talk. I'm not going to tell people and make this a community conversation." If that organization had gone through those kinds of trials, there was already enough trash on the street. I didn't need to add to it.

I had a learning in that box with the binder that I've never forgotten. There were reports and minutes of meetings held, especially one meeting a month before I was hired. It was a board meeting and Helen was there. She was asked to go out in the hallway for part of the meeting, and she took notes on everything that was said because she could hear the board from out in the hallway. I remember my jaw dropped and I thought, "Now I know why I was hired."

Up to this point, I thought I was joining a new organization as a first-time executive director. Nobody told me any differently, and I didn't know what had gone on. It turns out that a board member wanted to get rid of the executive director; she in turn wanted to get rid of them; and of course they got into conflict. She eavesdropped, wrote out what was said, and sent it in to the national office. She discredited the name and demanded the national office yank their membership. And that left a board where half of them were for her, and half of them were against her.

There were ten people on the board list at the time. Only five were at the board meeting, and the rest resigned. At the time I was thinking, "This is a piece of work." What I learned and had never encountered before is that I came face-to-face with people who turned away from me, wouldn't acknowledge me, and wouldn't speak to me. Some board members shut me out and shut me down. They were entirely new people in my space. Strangers. I had never experienced that before.

The truth is that every organization has skeletons in its closet. A history of unfortunate events. People who don't agree and don't get along. Conflict in various forms. Obstacles at every turn. Who are you in the matter? How you approach it and interact with it is a big predictor of your current results.

Thriving Point:

As an executive director, approach your role and your job with a singular attitude—*just do it.*

How do you approach and conduct difficult conversations in your organization?

THE TRUTH IS nobody in a nonprofit has been trained in human resources unless they walk in the door with a background in it, either through schooling or previous job experience. For most executive directors, the skill and experience just isn't there, and it certainly wasn't there for me. Early on, I discovered that asking board members for HR advice turned into a disaster every time. So, I had to learn on the job...just like you.

About midway through my 30-year career, I had developed a style. My willingness to confront difficult conversations was always there, but my finesse in actually executing them evolved over time. Most of my difficult conversations were with staff and volunteers.

What I found over the years is that people tend to define difficult conversations in the same way. In your average workplace, if a staff member is digging their own work-related grave, so to speak, someone in the vicinity will gladly push them all the way in. Even a manager or a colleague will do it. The approach is something along the lines of, "I need to tell an under-performing staff member they're doing a bad job. I need to make them feel badly so they'll turn it around." But really, who wants to do that? Nobody I can think of. Particularly in a nonprofit where most everyone's primary focus is doing as much good as they can.

I'm inviting you to define difficult conversations entirely differently from this point forward. Nowadays, the question I ask myself is, "How do I help someone turn themselves right side up?" They will or they won't, and I want to give them a chance to do the right thing. Because really, they know what is right and they know what to do. They don't need my (or your) help with that.

I had a staff who, when hired, was incredibly promising. This 40-ish high energy woman had one really big thing to offer: she understood the clients of an organization like ours. She had a rough upbringing, went to work at age 12, was living on her own at 13, and was pregnant at 16. She had the blueprint of all the kinds of things that can occur in life, and Boys & Girls Club's Mission is to step in and fill some of those gaps. Unfortunately however, she didn't have the support of an organization like Boys & Girls Club growing up.

When this spitfire woman was hired, she *got* the cause. Although she previously worked in retail, she immediately brought the soul of the Mission into her work. It was really exciting because we didn't have to explain much to her. She just got it. She knew what our kids go through because she had been one of them. We did all kinds of skill-building to equip her with everything she needed to succeed at her new job.

We were two years into her employment full time. And then something changed with our golden girl. She started to unravel. She got an attitude. She got mouthy and disrespectful. She started rolling her eyes and acting like she didn't care about things. We ignored it for a while. We certainly saw it, but it wasn't like every day was a bad day. Still, it would show up. We made it through the summer, and she was in a key role the entire time. She delivered, but the spirit of her work had changed.

In situations like this, I didn't jump out and look in

the back pocket of people's personal lives. That wasn't my role. But given that kind of remarkable difference, it was clear something in her world had changed. Sure enough, I found out something was happening in her personal life, and it was building. Eventually I took the program director aside and told her it had to be dealt with. As much as we valued this staff member, this new version of her was intolerable.

I sat down with this once valued and cherished staff member and the program director. "We're at a fork in the road," I said. "This is not a conversation I wanted to have, but you've brought us here. I want you to listen to what I've heard you say that tells me you no longer want this job." I went down the list I had in front of me point by point. She cried. "Do you agree with any of those points?" I asked. She said yes. "I'll tell you what I'm going to do. You're going home now at noon. And you're not coming back until Monday at 9:00 am. You're not doing the event tomorrow. I have that covered. At 9:00 am on Monday, you come in prepared to tell me whether you plan to stay, or whether this is not for you. And then you'll get to ask me the same question. At the end of that meeting, we'll have a decision."

She left upset and shocked. It was a Friday, the day before the event where she was supposed to play a lead role. It was her favourite event of the year, and she had rented a costume specifically for it. She left the building that day, costume in hand. She was devastated. She was a kid at heart and she loved these events. It stirred her roots.

On Monday morning she came in. "So what is your decision?" I asked. She said, "I want to stay. I want this job. I love this job." I said, "Okay, now we're going to look at a document together. I'm putting you on probation for

90 days." I outlined the terms of her probation. At any time during the 90 days, either one of us could exercise our right to terminate her job. It was a difficult conversation, but had I not done it, she would've continued to sour the environment. She would've continued to be a non-team player.

It was three weeks after that we sat down. The first 14 days of her probation were great. She behaved as she had when she was first hired. Then we had a long weekend with a holiday thrown in. Upon returning from that weekend, her old pre-probation-self showed up to work. I let her go shortly after.

Now, I was a notoriously challenging person to work for. The level at which I worked was higher than most, but the people who worked for me rose to the occasion. Not only was it who I was; it was who they were. They had just never tapped into it before they met me. I suppose it would've been easy for my staff to loathe me and my standards, but I made it impossible for them to do that. Because I gave them a choice to rise.

The people who worked for me thrived, particularly those who had a great work ethic and fell in love with the race. There were others whom I knew underneath were struggling on some level, but they could not ignore the latitude I gave them. They couldn't ignore the acknowledgment they got unexpectedly, or the trust they were given just by showing up every day to work. I frequently said to new staff, "Anyone in this building will tell you that where I start is, I trust you until you take it away. That's my only rule." They'd probably never heard it before. The rest of the world expects you to earn their trust. In the organization where I was executive director, you could either build your own castle or dig your own grave.

If we truly want to lead, we need to stop throwing away human beings. Instead, we need to trust people who are unraveling to manage themselves. How I did that was by calling a meeting. Before the conversation, I spent time thinking and listening as if I were them. What told me I have to call this meeting? I listed it out and thought about how to put it on the table so they wouldn't just hear it; they would own it.

When they came in, they weren't expecting what was coming, but by the time I laid down the issues, they knew. In fact, deep down they knew before they walked in. I provided real examples to bring it into their reality. Then there was that moment when they were clearly in the center of the conversation, and there was a fork in the road. I gave them a choice to step in or step out. I gave them the freedom to do the right thing for them.

Thriving Point:

To redefine the difficult conversations you must have inside your organization, you must redefine how you lead.

How are you showing up for your staff as a nonprofit leader?

IT'S A DIFFERENT SPIRIT and a different expectation to work for a nonprofit. It's not for everyone. The work you do is important, and you must pick up your head when someone walks in because you are there to serve. You must be willing to connect. The truth is you don't know what the outcome of a connection is going to be. You have to be willing to be stretched to a new place, because that is what it takes for success.

Whenever we posted new positions at the organization where I served as executive director, I watched for responsiveness, thoroughness, and how they showed up. If we invited a person in, what was their response time? How a person showed up told me how important this was. That includes where they parked, how they walked, their eyes, and many other nonverbal signals. If a person parked in front of the door, it was probably not going to be a fit. Because there's more in the world than just you. First impressions tell me what I can build on and what I have to fix as a leader. Truthfully, the further along on this path I went, the less I even *wanted* to fix. I was mindful that people had to be rewarded for their efforts. I didn't get caught up with diplomas and academics. I was looking for life skills and hard skills, and I had a commitment to retaining people so they made this a career.

I was masterful at nudging people to do what they could do. I did it from morning to night. We'd bring a new person in and another staff would tell them, "You will be stretched more than you've ever been stretched in your life. Sheree will ask you to do things and you'll think—no, but you'll do it anyway." It's just the way it was. I never thought it was stretching. It's just what we did. Over 90% of the people out there are in dead town.

My number one mantra as executive director? "When you're in, you're on." I said that to everyone. If you stepped foot in our building and the phone rang, or somebody came in, and supposedly "we aren't open yet," **We are open because you're here.** Yes, you had to lock yourself away at times to do good work. But if it was a Sunday afternoon and you were on my staff, and you chose to come in and get some extra work done, and that phone rang, that phone got answered. I always lived this way, and it's how my staff lived too. We never knew who is going to take us to the next level. People come in all sizes, shapes, and ages and at all times of day and night. You don't know who has magic in them that you can't see.

My number two mantra as executive director? "You start it, you finish it." I was all for multi-tasking and being busy. However, when staff had their hand on something, they had to know there was someone else's hand that was coming right behind them, so they needed to leave it in a state to be passed on. They were not the only person in the organization, and everyone needed to know the trail. When staff started something and couldn't finish it or they were going home, they left a note with their initials and the date, because we wanted continuity in our service and communications. When Ron came in, I wanted to be able to speak to him based on the notes left by staff. Not "Oh gee, Ann's not here. She'll have to get back to you." There is only *now*. And that's a skill I taught, because not everyone has that.

One of the things I did was take four or five of my

staff at a time to go see our partner organizations in other communities. We gave those organizations a heads-up so they knew we're coming. What I know is you only have an appreciation for what you have if you see something different. I wanted staff to go visit and see if there was something we could do differently or something they could add. The organizations we visited may have had something more than we did, but they also may not have had everything we did. My staff came to appreciate having lots of tools and flexibility. And they loved how they were empowered to do the work they did every day. I believed in developing staff, and I invested in them to get those skills.

Thriving Point:

The mantras you speak have an impact on the way your staff shows up every day. Choose your words and phrases wisely, for they make those around you grow or shrink.

How are you leading your board when it comes to overhead?

THERE IS NO DOUBT the boardroom is an intimidating environment. All the various personalities arrive, and it influences how you think and how you act as an executive director, because it's your job and they have power. It's a vulnerable environment and it can become volatile quickly. A board is tasked with creating the policies and holding the organization accountable. However, most board members come from the for-profit world. When they get inside a nonprofit, the measurement stick is very different and many board members pull back and proclaim, "don't waste money." They want low budget/high performance, and that's a false model. This shows up in many ways, including hiring staff and investing in marketing.

When I was first hired as executive director we were in an office that had 28 steps straight up. The door unlocked at the sidewalk level and there were two other offices upstairs besides ours. I got there one Monday morning, and to my surprise, I didn't have to unlock the door on the sidewalk level. I arrived at the top of the stairs and there was a woman standing close to my office door. She introduced herself as Wendy and I invited her in.

Wendy was all dressed up and she said, "I'm here to work." I said, "Oh, where?" She said, "I'm here to work at Big Brothers Big Sisters." I said, "Oh, great!" Up to this point, I had been working alone. I found out later that Wendy was sent to me on a six-month employment grant from a politician. No one called me and told me, but I was thrilled to have her.

Wendy was my first co-worker and administrative assistant. I was grateful, and didn't even question it. She stayed for the first few years of growth in the organization, and was a big part of our success. I still consider it one of the best days of my life when she showed up to work and we were still figuring it out. She created systems for us. We didn't know what we didn't know, and she had a wonderful spirit. If you could hand-pick your perfect employee, Wendy was it.

This began what I refer to as the "mobile phase" of my tenure as executive director. The year was 1987 and the mobile phase lasted through 1996. Why the mobile phase? Because we lived out of bins and moved offices continuously. If there was a place to rent that was $40 cheaper, we moved. When someone joined our board who felt like they had a better spot and influenced the decision, we moved again. Those moves were brutal and led by volunteers. The board table alone weighed about 600 pounds. I'll never forget one of our most loyal volunteers who said to me, "Look, I've moved you guys three times. Next time, don't call me. I can't do this anymore." We were exactly what we appeared to be. A roving nonprofit to save money.

Besides facilitating our programs by putting them into a bin and meeting people at the corner store, we also did our hiring that way. We never had the money to hire the person of our choice. What we did have was the openness to accept people who would come by way of an employment grant. Which meant we often didn't get to choose, because the grant to employ the person was meeting their needs, not ours.

What I didn't know at the time is that when a person

comes to be hired and they have their funding with them, there's a reason. They were referred to us based on chronic unemployment or some kind of workplace adapting issues. They were matched with us. We could certainly have turned it down. However, the combination of the need for the work to get done and the funding provided meant we were much more open to making it work. We weren't looking for the best person at that time. We were simply thankful we didn't have to fundraise in order to hire people.

When the six months ended, out the door they went. And I needed to get another grant to get another person. This eventually became a problem. Of course we had high turnover — new people every six months! There was no continuity in skill and training. It was a time investment we had to make over and over again, and it was clearly unsustainable.

The sad reality is that many nonprofit boards become addicted to short-term staff and no results. I lived this for my first five or six years as executive director. Board members are not on-site day to day to see what it's like. It's tough to start with someone new every 26 weeks and teach them how to answer the phone and where to put the mail. As a new executive director, I wanted to be successful and didn't want to rock the boat. Eventually, however, I discovered how hard this staffing predicament was to manage.

There is a root issue in all nonprofits, which is high turnover and poor-quality work. Both stem from how a nonprofit is measured and what the expectation is. There is a moral misjudgment around what the money is for in a nonprofit. People ask, "How much are you spending on staffing?" and "How much are you spending on marketing?" Well, you know something? They miss the point that every dollar that comes into this organization is to meet the Mission. We don't just slice out a pie and say, "That's overhead." What do you think the overhead is for?

In fact, an executive director has to spin a wheel with various spokes, starting with marketing, human resources, programs, planning and finance. There are five or six spokes to be managed, and your typical executive director is likely not trained or experienced in any more than perhaps two of them. So when the spirit of the board was, "Don't waste money", my response was, "Well, what would you like me to do?" If this was a for-profit business, this thing called overhead wouldn't even be a question. Assuming you make good choices, the more resources you invest in what you do, the more success you will have.

Thriving Point:

Train and develop your board in the idea that the more you invest in resources, the more your success comes—because the mindset of getting everything for free is false.

How do you navigate the blame game?

THE ROLE OF EXECUTIVE DIRECTOR invites an easy and prime target for people to place blame, either intentionally or unintentionally. I see this play out in two ways.

Firstly, I see people intentionally blaming an executive director. When an executive director tries to move people to a place where they are accountable and take responsibility for themselves, and there's an unwillingness or resistance by that person, they blame the executive director. Secondly, I see executive directors being either insecure or trying to please many masters, walking that tightrope between board and staff. And that "aloneness" factor often accepts or offers to take the blame when, in fact, that's not the issue.

As an executive director, you're going to be blamed even if you had nothing to do with the situation in question. You have to get comfortable with taking the high road; if you don't, you are never going to win. When situations hit you, as they always do, you might think, "It's not like that," or "That's not the way things went down." You have to step outside of it, or you'll be drawn into battles you can't win, and fight situations that are a waste of your time.

When I served as executive director, I had a situation with a staff whom I put on probation. She ended up resigning her position, but I'm sure she wouldn't have resigned if she hadn't gone on probation. Instead of saying, "I don't want to work here anymore, so I'm resigning," she most certainly blamed me because I put her on probation. I was the easy mark.

When a troublesome incident arises, your reaction as an executive director can easily make it worse. It's easy to slide right down to that low level, which is reactive, at which point you start having very basic thoughts that are not for the team, and not for the good of the work. Side conversations begin, and people start seeing allies and loyalties. A negative culture builds up in the organization and derails everyone on their own issues. Fear starts to seep in, and misinformation runs wild.

Most executive directors find human resources difficult. Many shops do not have HR expertise or counsel on site, so you're often thrown into a fire that you need to fight armed with not much more than your best intentions. And those best intentions mean you will have to render a decision that isn't easy, isn't going to land well, and is going to affect another human being. Here again, you must rise above it and say, "I'm doing what the job involves, the work needs, and the Mission requires. I'm prepared to make a decision that can include termination, probation, or a long period of recalibrating someone to do the work they need to do." You can't ignore it, or hope it goes away or fixes itself, or pray that they see the light. Those things won't solve themselves in the normal course of events without your direct, personal intervention. And when you intervene, you have to assume that you will likely be blamed.

Aside from issues with staff, many executive directors blame the board, which is obviously part of decision-making. They're in the room when decisions get made and they understand the context and the background. But too often when an executive director communicates an issue to staff, they blame the board. The board is their shield. Executive directors are notorious for blaming their board for tough decisions they knew had to be done.

One thing that is so interesting about the boardroom is that as an executive director, you insist on a unified board. You've likely decided that's important, but the truth is, you have to pick your battles. There are many games you can play: it can be either the game of winning the organization's Mission, or the game of winning a battle against someone who is blaming you. In fact, most executive directors play the wrong game. You know the truth or the why, and you want to get that on the table … even though no-one is listening and no-one is interested.

You're always going to have a trail of vocal, unsupportive, and blaming people. They are there, and they are also not your donor, your supporter or your volunteer. They are the 20% who, regardless of what acrobatics you go through, will not engage. It's not easy to rise above it, but that's the difference between winning and fighting. You're not winning when you are fighting the wrong issue.

There are two common situations that happen most often when it comes to executive directors. The first is you leave quickly. You leave after a year and a half or two, before these kinds of situations have to be dealt with. The second is you suffer and wish it were different. And you have a long line of people — 30% of whom are toxic, chaotic, disruptive, not pulling the mission forward — and you tolerate it. And you are terminally unhappy because of it. Which one are you?

Thriving Point:

As an executive director, your problem isn't that your board made a decision without you, and it isn't that your staff is blaming you. Your problem is you aren't willing to make decisions and stand up for them, regardless of where the blame might fall.

As a leader of a nonprofit, how do you cultivate capable staff?

———————— ⁕ ————————

WORKING WITH STAFF is the same as working with the board. If you show and teach people how things work, they'll rise to a new level of understanding and capability. If all they hear from you are phrases like, "that's not in the budget," it's time to take a step back. You don't understand your role as executive director.

Using the budget example, teach your staff what that means. And more importantly, how does "it" get in the budget in the first place? That's the real question. Everybody leads from, "that's not in the budget" and "we can't afford it." Spend some time with your staff so they understand how that budget was built. Then, when something is not in it, they'll understand why.

There is never enough time spent with staff on why things are the way they are. This absence of context is dominant in all organizations because everyone is racing down the hall with no time to spare. You'll save a lot of time, however, if you help someone learn the why, and give them the context so they can figure it out. That's what is missing. Instead of saying to your staff, "We have to do X and Y," bring them into it. Teach them to think things through and give them responsibility. If you're going to ask someone for money, bring your staff into the decision or the need that is there, and give them some ownership.

I always talked about the gap. I always said, "As a staff person, you're here to fill in the gap." If we wanted to do a food drive and we wanted 2000 crates of food donated,

I asked them, "When are you going to have it done, and how many people do you need to do it?" I started to break it down, and then had them take it from there. Typically I'd say, "we need X," and leave it to them to come up with the solution and the "how to". Then they would have their own little road map with signposts telling them how to get there. Unfortunately, however, most humans don't think that way. They need to be walked and talked into a process. People ask me, "How did you do all that?" I did it on the front end.

I said to Whitney, "You say we're going to do 80 mentoring matches by December. Go away and bring me back what the number is going to be at the end of each month, at the end of September, October and November. Bring me back the numbers." She came back with her numbers and they were very realistic. I said, "Great. So you have two weeks to get to that first 46. Sketch out your plan of where you're going to hit with an ask, and what you need the marketing person to do, and how often you need them to do it." On the 21st of September, I checked in with her. I said, "Next week is the end of our month. You said you would be at 45. Are we on track?" She was at 47. She had already made her goal.

Cultivating staff requires breaking things down, creating the architecture, and helping them see where they are in it. Many people spend time drifting around in their head because they're not sure and they don't know. Also, people have a tendency to spend all their time on the final outcome instead of the milestones to get there. They never define step one, so they never arrive anywhere.

The ugly truth is there is something people rarely learn on the street, and they rarely learn at home, which is how to *think*. The education system isn't teaching it, so you end up with employees who really don't know how to work. They don't naturally know how to set and achieve goals. There is an automatic assumption made that people know how to do this. I assure you, they don't.

Thriving Point:

Become the leader who cultivates the ability to *think* in your staff.

Mindful
and
Deliberate
Board Management

What must you do when you get the wrong person on the board?

—————————◆◆◆◆—————————

THIS HAPPENS OFTEN because there is always a need on charity boards, and there is often a rush to fill seats. You don't have time on your side, so you take shortcuts in your eagerness and the need to fill a seat. I lived through three agonizing situations as an executive director when board members had to be removed. We were willing to roll up our sleeves and do it, but it was painful.

This particular topic is usually dodged, ignored and denied. What's unique about it, is if you own a company and you've got someone causing a problem, you have that one meeting that solves the problem: "This is the way the door swings." But when you have a board, you've got to be a real warrior to take them on. A board member typically has a three-year term, but if they have one year, you must still have the will to act.

Good governance insists that a board has a development committee (or nominating committee). In my organization, we had a development committee of three, and they dealt with three particular issues. The purpose of the committee is to fill the seats at the board table, but the real role of the board development committee, its really crucial task, is to work with the board throughout the year, and resolve "issues" that come up. That's an insight I only grasped in my third decade as an executive director. I thought they had a job once or twice a year: "The annual meeting is coming; get the names on the slate." And that is indeed historically and traditionally what they do. But in fact they have a much deeper and broader role—to manage tough issues that arise within the board itself.

Most executive directors suffer in silence over this issue. I had the good fortune to work with many great board members over the years, but sometimes you have a board of all nut cases. And in fact, there is no perfect board; there'll always be one or two people who are not the best fit.

It's like having five children. Three are shining stars. They do everything to be helpful, cooperative, and productive. And then you've got one who's lazy and doesn't care about school. And the last one who is just determined to destroy. Those kids grow older, and one way or another, they end up on boards. They don't really get the Mission, and if you were to ask them why they are there, they would say, "I don't know."

Every board ends up with someone whose personality is argumentative. It's their personal style no matter what the issue, and they'll always take the other side. There is certainly room for the devil's advocate, but there also has to be a cooperative spirit. So when it comes to argumentative types, you tolerate them and try to guide them. Give them some boundaries. An argumentative personality is not a reason to remove someone. It's simply a difficult voice in the boardroom. A challenge indeed, but at its best, it will sometimes force the board to confront an important issue it was overlooking.

It's a very different circumstance, however, when you have someone on the board who is not for the Mission. Sometimes you miss it at first, but generally they have zero interest in what you do. They may be there for personal reasons—a promotion, a better résumé, or prestige. Little more than a warm body. Most boards can tolerate it as long as they don't offer resistance. And they usually don't, because they are usually there for self-gain. But they also can't be relied on. You can't count on them to do the right thing for the Mission because they're there for themselves first. That's very frustrating, and these people do turn up on boards regularly.

It's when you get a really difficult person who either has an agenda or needs control and wants to drive the bus that you have a tougher nut to crack. Even if you discover it early, you need to let time do its thing. You need evidence. It's like a fire. You smell the smoke early, but you can't act until you're sure they have an agenda. And then you have to figure out what that agenda is.

Obviously, you can't just go out and knock people off the board randomly because "this is where I think this is going." Time is necessary for you to have your proof that a person is behaving like your sixth sense is telling you. And it must be a significant issue — not a personality clash. So how do you handle it?

Once you have clarified a real issue, put it on the table with the board chair. Let's say you have a clear and recent instance of the counterproductive behaviour. You can say to the board chair, "What did you think when _____?" or "How did you feel about _____?" and see if the board chair shares your take on it. If they don't, you need more time. Because if you're right and this person has an agenda, it will continue to play out. Time will tell. You've got to wait again for another experience or another moment when this person goes in that direction again. The next time it happens and the next time you meet with your board chair, ask them, "At such and such meeting when X happened, were you surprised?" You have to elicit from your board chair either a shared or a contrary view, because there may be a view you haven't considered yet, and that is valuable.

If your issue is a serious one, it could be affecting many things: even the relationship between the executive director and the board itself. It could be a bottom-line issue around funding. It could be affecting dynamics in the boardroom. It could be affecting just getting the work done. At this point you need a conversation with key people on the board you trust. You need objective, tough, and critical thinkers, not people who would respond to your concern with, "Oh well, I don't think he's like that," or "No I don't think she'd ever do that." This is not the mind you want to connect with. You want people who will listen critically to the issues you raise to determine if they have a point of view that is consistent with where you see this going.

By the time you've spoken with a second, third or fourth person about the issue, the question will come up: What are we going to do about this? Either a board member or the executive director will raise it. And then you'll need a plan that includes five things:

1. What are we dealing with?

2. How are we going to do it?

3. Who's going to be in the room?

4. When are we doing it?

5. What does the next day look like?

It is the execution of this plan that removes a person who is clearly wrong for the board.

Thriving Point:

An ultimately successful organization requires the timely removal of board members who are a threat to the organization, whether they are there for personal gain or are just going against the Mission.

Who is the cast of characters in your boardroom?

IN EVERY NONPROFIT, your board is like a cast of characters. Their name badge tells you what to call them, and their seat at the table has an indelible name. The seats have themes. Different people sit in those seats, and the theme shows up in how they behave and what they bring to the board.

There's always a swivel chair on the board. It's typically a revolving door, and people move in and out of that chair on a consistent basis. It's the seat you have to keep filling because it's where the problem shows up. Sometimes you know ahead of time; other times it can't be predicted.

One seat will always have a person who can't get beyond their own reality — Sally Stuck. They may work in a very controlled environment such as government. They typically have a controlled income line, so they live in a very linear, uninterrupted world. That's how they see the world, and on the board they're usually just confused. Unfortunately, however, when people are confused they tend to focus on the wrong issues.

When I was executive director, we had a woman on the board who had served previously on the board back when we were struggling. She returned during what I will call "the glory days," so she found a very different dynamic in the boardroom. She had a group of friends who were always peppering her with questions about the organization. I told her she needed to get new friends — because she lived in a very linear, insulated world. She was a perfect example of the seat of a person on the board who can't get past their own reality.

There's always a seat held by someone who deals in the end goal or big goal — Dolly Dreamer. They live 30,000 feet up at the peak of the mountain, and that's where their thinking is. They have value but sometimes you have to bring them down a little closer to the real world.

There are always the peacekeepers — Pleasant Peter. Reliable and comfortable, they'll often make up about one-third of the board. They sit in the middle of the boat and enjoy the ride. They know where we're going, but they may not be doing a great deal to help you get there. They're like the choir. They know the song; they always show up; and you can generally count on them.

And then there is the rogue seat — Roger Ruthless. This could also be the swivel chair. They only like rough waters or crisis situations and are usually looking for something to probe and poke. High maintenance, their management will consume much of your energy and attention. They are demanding, prone to error, loud, and often selfish.

There's the good Samaritan who wants to do really good work — Paula Passion. Whatever it takes, they roll up their sleeves and get it done. They are astute and more active and vocal than the peacekeepers.

And there's the helper, kind and well-intentioned but with no board experience — Harriet Helper. She shows up for every meeting and every event with a great smile and always kind words. But she's way out of her league. There are other roles in the organization for Harriet Helper. When tasked with board governance, fundraising and stewardship, Harriet Helper just smiles more.

Others may show up at your board table. You might have a Strategy Sam who gets it, sees the big picture, feels the Mission and wisely stays out of the kitchen. A good seatmate for Sam is Marilyn Marketer. They make a great team. Sam articulates the need and Marilyn makes a motion to invest the money in getting the message out. She reminds the board to put the face on the Mission.

That's your typical board cast of characters.

Whoever else may be on your board, however, it's essential to have someone who understands money and what money can do. There are too many examples of boards that are sitting on an endowment, for example, and doing nothing with it. An endowment does no good if it's not being directed. And there are too many boards looking at deficits and nodding "Okay." It's not okay. A deficit is a symptom of deeper problems and someone at the board table has to start that conversation. That's why you want someone on your board who understands money and what it can do, and who can speak to financial issues. Inexperience and avoidance are root causes of struggling nonprofits. Preserving and fixating on the assets is not the goal of a nonprofit.

Thriving Point:

Knowing and understanding your board's cast of characters tells you where your strengths and weaknesses lie as an organization. Too much of one or more characters tips the boat.

What is your board and staff's relation to the budget?

LESS THAN ONE-THIRD of any group of board members truly understands a budget. Put a balance sheet, a revenue and expense statement, or a profit and loss statement in front of them and they disconnect. While we've moved on from a world where very few people balance their checkbook, we've entered an electronic world where no-one keeps a receipt. Putting numbers of any significant size and scope in front of people and expecting them to have a point of view on it is almost impossible.

As an executive director facing this challenge I created a *Program Budget*. Instead of overhead line items such as heat, light, rent, mowing, etc., I took every separate program we wanted to offer and created a budget that plugged in every *direct* cost associated with that program. Every overhead expense had a percentage allocated out to each of the specific programs we were offering. And then I pitched the specific program to the board. In the overall organization budget, you didn't see a line item that read "food" because there was a percentage of the cost of food allocated to each of the programs.

Once the organization shifted to what I called *Program Budgeting*, they got it. Some items in a nonprofit have a hefty price tag and are outside the scope of what most people would realize. Items such as postage and marketing are the kinds of costs that make board members ask, "Is that really necessary?" That question gets answered clearly and simply, however, as soon as you tie it directly to an outcome, the impact and the benefit.

Boards and executive directors fall down when they look at a one-pager with random line items and dollars plugged in, and make a judgment based on their own life experience. "Oh, in my business, I'd never spend that much on marketing", they tend to say. To which my response is, "Maybe you wouldn't, but this is not about *your* business."

A Program Budget allowed us to have a really robust budget. For years, we put money into the budget for marketing, whereas in most nonprofits, that's a non-starter because it looks like excess, a frill. The other item as unpopular as marketing costs is training and professional development. And that's exactly why there is so much churn in nonprofit staffing and retention is so low. Money is rarely invested in training staff and giving them opportunities to learn and get new ideas. Unfortunately, that is what ignites the desire in an employee to leave a job.

Under my Program Budget system, we looked at every program we wanted to offer in the coming year and put costs on all the pieces — staffing, fuel, whatever. I said, "If you want to reach 200 clients with this program, this is the price tag." An example was our ZigZag summer camp program.

I would ask the program director, "How long will it run?" Three months. "What do you need to be successful?" A vehicle, fuel, a pop-up tent, tables, ice, and so on. "Let's picture what all the things that are going to happen on the ground are going to look like." And then I would say, "Okay, we've got about 29 different line items here. How many days are you going out for?" Thirty days. "How much is fuel going to be per week?" We plugged in all the numbers, totaled it, and it came to around $65,000. The program director was stunned.

My next question would be, "How many kids are you going to be sure are there?" Fifty. Then, "Okay, so we're going to have 50 kids daily for 30 days. We're going to reach 1500 kids. Push that into your total cost. Now, how much is it costing you per day to offer ZigZag to a child?" And we had a number. Her response, "I didn't realize all this. I never thought about the numbers." I said, "Well that's helpful, because now when you pour out the juice instead of keeping it, you'll understand you're pouring our money down the drain. When you forget all the art supplies at the tent and come back, that's an unnecessary expense you just created for us."

And that was a critical insight for all our staff to grasp: if we used our money well, we could do more. It created a culture in the organization, and the entire staff understood it well. It's how the organization did business when I led as executive director.

Thriving Point:

The key to inspiring your board and getting a budget approved is to wrap the budget in tangible numbers that include all costs tied directly to programs and services. Money for the Mission must be packaged in outcomes.

Should organizations rely on board members to open doors?

Universally, nonprofits seem to operate with an expectation along the lines of, "If we get Paul on the board, he will open more doors for us." But I don't think that's how it happens. Not even close.

The board is the doorway to your organization, not the other way around. Those nine to twelve people are the doorway into your organization from the community. They come from all walks of life and each brings their own different experiences and viewpoints, many of them valuable to the organization. But the worst of all reasons to bring someone on the board is so they can open doors for you.

"Opening doors" is a cliché touted in boardrooms and fraught with false hopes, misplaced vision and turmoil. If that's the main filter used in selecting a person for your board, expect a ride on a runaway roller coaster. Why? Because you sought them for their connections rather than their personal commitment. They will likely open doors, but not necessarily the right doors for you.

Wealth. Status. Success. Those are the desired attributes everyone talks about when they look around for new board members. There's a price for that, and it gets exacted in the boardroom and spills into the office of the executive director. When you have too many people who are perceived as door-openers, you'll quickly find yourself in a minefield. You never know whose real agenda is dressed up and cloaked with suave comments. There are always two channels to every conversation: one is what they are saying; the other is their unspoken intent.

A board member brought on to open doors can use that role as a bargaining chip, and you'll certainly get behaviours based on their personal equity. They may want the organization to go in a certain direction that feeds *their* agenda rather than yours. They may want to do this or that that has little or nothing to do with your Mission, but they'll smoothly present it as such. And they won't make an introduction unless you twist your programs so that something is done a certain way — their way. While there's no questioning the importance of connections or denying their very significant *potential* value to the organization, it has to be done with integrity.

Jack was a well-known door-opener, and his business was hugely successful. He was sought after for boards, and he had made the rounds. He was on the hospital board and the church board and when he spoke, all heads turned his way. And he was used to that treatment in the boardroom.

Then he was invited to a small nonprofit board. Jack the door-opener was a big catch for this little shop. For a while, he sat back and listened, but it didn't take long until he began to meddle, undermine and control. How did this show up? When he offered to chair a key fund-raising project and took the project outside the organization. He turned his back on the fundraising staff, the board chair and other board members. It was his show, and it was orchestrated in the backroom of his office. He assembled his team, withheld information and gave selective updates at the board meeting.

It eventually became obvious that Jack's real end goal was to undermine the executive director, and in the process he subtly created chaos inside the organization.

Successful, powerful, authoritative — that was Jack. The executive director soon realized the door should have been slammed and bolted when Jack came up the path. He was a narcissist…a solo renegade.

Door-openers are rarely team players, and a board, if it is to be successful, must be a team. Once inside the boardroom, the door-opener director too often shows up as a rogue board member. Instead of living in a world of consensus, their ego drives them to fly solo. Their competitive dog-eat-dog world is one of connections with payoffs and tip-offs to leverage their agenda. People in their path are often trampled.

So what makes them door-openers? Because some human beings crave attention, seek adulation, and climb the ladder to perceived success at any cost. Meanwhile there are always plenty of bystanders and wannabes to bless them with the aura of door-opener. These types are often recruited to lead major fundraising campaigns, and if they aren't the lead role, they often round out the team organizing the campaign or event.

One such door-opener was Karen. During a duck race fundraising event, she lost her canoe paddle, and she was furious. Amid her lost canoe paddle chaos, the boom broke during the race and all the ducks got away. The race was cancelled, and no winner was determined. There was angst, backlash, disappointment and frustration, and the aftermath was awful.

Core volunteers rolled up their sleeves, salvaged the ducks as they headed to the bay, and worked through the night to clean up the project. The next morning, staff and volunteers huddled to sort out what to do next, in the midst of which Karen came barging through the door, hysterical and demanding her lost canoe paddle or $500 to replace it by 4:00 p.m. The executive director tried to calm her with no luck. She called at 4:05 p.m. No paddle. And no, she would not be getting $500.

The next door that Karen opened was her husband's. He called the board chair, and at the same time, a letter came through the fax machine on their company letterhead addressed to the board seeking $500 or the paddle. So at the next board meeting, the paddle wrath had everyone's attention. The outcome: no paddle was found, there was no payment of $500 to Karen, and the other "door-opener" on the board, Betty, resigned in support of Karen. There was an offer to Karen. Bob had a few extra paddles in his shed and he offered her one. Karen turned it down. The truth is, it wasn't about the paddle. It was that Karen went through life esteemed as a door-opener and doors opened in her presence. This didn't happen this time, and she made sure she slammed doors closed.

It's easy to step over people who could do good work and offer good solutions. There is some kind of filter people have collectively agreed is the best one, and they measure it with their success, their standing, and their wealth. It's the wrong approach.

Thriving Point:

Let your board be a representative cross section of the talent, skill and expertise in your community, a group that is willing and able to serve your organization's Mission powerfully vs. opening doors.

How does your board know where it's going?

Have you noticed in board meetings how easy it is to talk about what's already happened…instead of where you're headed? I found myself struggling with exactly that several years ago, particularly when the organization where I served as executive director exploded as the result of the success of a fundraising initiative called Gold Rush. Shortly after that I introduced the *dashboard* into board meetings.

When you sit down in your car and turn on the engine, the dashboard in front of you tells you the status of your vehicle. I wanted our board to have a one-page document — a *board dashboard* — so that as they walked into a meeting they knew the key issues. Our dashboard told the board what the key indicators were, what they needed to deal with, and where the organization was right then. Seven categories gave them a synopsis, background and insights so they could ask questions with context.

If you're in a typical nonprofit, chances are good that your board walks into meetings and looks at the past. What already happened? They often come together to acknowledge what has been done, keep their heads down, and never look at the future. Unfortunately, this means that they are often sideswiped with something they could have predicted had they been dealing with the upcoming issues. Too many board members, as a result, tend to walk out of board meetings thinking, "That was such a waste of time!" And then they return the next month and do it all over again!

Our dashboard told us where we were, the speed we were going, how much fuel we had, how far we'd gone, what risks we were facing, and what was happening that was going to affect us. The very last question we asked at every board meeting was, "What should we be thinking about?" And that's a really courageous question, because you don't know what or how challenging the responses are going to be when you throw that out. The board chair asked the question and threw the meeting wide open for discussion. It did two things. It gave anyone with something meaningful to contribute a chance to do so, and it gave an ordinarily silent member some comfort in knowing that if and when they did have an issue someday, they would be heard. That's where they could say it. So it was a very interesting question.

Over the years, that last question from the board chair generated some interesting responses. Sometimes they were well thought out; sometimes not; and other times they were game-changing. An example was when a board member said, "When I look at society and I see these changes in our lifestyles and families, I think our organization has a role in mental health with children. Not counseling, not one-to-one, not a therapeutic thing. What can we be doing for the mental health wellness of all the children who pass through our doors or who need this kind of help?"

That very thought expressed by that board member was the catalyst for a program for kids in grades 3 and 4. Out of the blue and unplanned. A robust program that ultimately had powerful impact and was fully endorsed by local schools. The seed was planted for this program when the board member had both the freedom and the opportunity to pose a question.

Dashboards pull all the key information into a one-pager. Use a dashboard to inform, gauge, probe, challenge, question, and create linkages. And then follow it up by ending every board meeting with the most powerful question of them all: *What should we be thinking about?*

Thriving Point:

Always rely on a dashboard in your nonprofit for driving questions and decisions.

How do you go about achieving trust with your board and board chair?

FOR AN EXECUTIVE DIRECTOR, there is no room for being vague, indecisive or unsure with your board. You can't waffle. You can't speak before you think, and then retract it and change your mind. You only have one chance in that meeting, and you have to be *on*. Indecision is the weakness that will take you down.

There are ten or more people sitting there in front of you. If you waffle, they'll poke holes in it, and they'll take you off your game. *You* led them there. Those are the moments where trust gets cracks in it, and they hang onto it because they're human, and humans hang onto the nitty gritty.

If a question gets asked and you give a vague answer, an eyebrow goes up. If there's a deadline you've committed to — for example, in July you said, "This is going to happen by August 15th" and in September the report shows that it hasn't happened — the *other* eyebrow goes up. Nothing gets said; it just gets noticed.

I have a sign that reads, "Sometimes silence is the best answer." That could just be a matter of catching your breath and collecting your thoughts. Use it when needed, because if you blurt something out it could haunt you. Be very deliberate. Let silence be your friend. At the same time, silence cannot run forever.

You build trust with your board by being accurate without being arrogant. Being very deliberate and very controlled. Kick the emotion to the curb. Nobody wants your hysteria. Nobody wants your woes. They want solid information so they know great things are happening. You're not sitting there complaining. You're proposing how this is gonna really work. Your board is not a sounding board for all the things that aren't working. The board meeting is not a time to cry over everything that went wrong. Money that didn't come in? Volunteers didn't respond? Control yourself. The board meeting is not a dirty laundry list of everything going wrong.

Building trust with your board chair begins with how you are positioned in the boardroom. They sit at the end of the boardroom table, and you sit in the seat immediately to their right at the table. You never give up that seat. You are there to support the board chair and to provide whatever he or she needs. As the rest of the board looks down the table, what they see before them is a team.

I've been in boardrooms where the board chair sits at one side of the table and the executive director sits at the opposite end. That's a nonverbal power trip. Adversarial for sure. If an executive director comes into the boardroom and pulls up the third chair from the center, I know they've forgotten their role. They've forgotten who they are.

As executive director, you need to be where the board chair is, and just to the side. The board meeting is not your show. You have a role in it, but you're not leading it. If you're doing your job properly, you've created a relationship with your board chair such that it makes sense for you to sit on their right. And it means something further that you sit to their right. The board chair relies on you for information. They rely on you for cue cards. You are their teleprompter. Make no mistake about it. The last thing you want is for your board chair to be on the spot without an answer, or caught off guard, or embarrassed. Once they start to unravel, that'll come into the boardroom in a big way.

Between board meetings, take a deeper dive into the key issues with your board chair. You want them to be prepared always, and never have an "Oh, I don't know" moment. They don't like surprises (no one does). They don't want to feel incompetent, and your role is to give them quality information at the right time so they are able to speak as the board chair. So many executive directors either don't understand this or ignore it. Make your board chair's job easy by being always open and honest with them. You can do that in person with quick conversations, or via email to say, "Heads up, this is coming. This is the action taken. This is the result. Just wanted you to know."

The pond I fished in as executive director was a small one, but I could always tell I had a new board chair by my interactions with them. If you asked anyone who served as board chair when I was executive director, they would say, "She looked after everything and she took care of everything." I suppose that's true...but maybe I just gave them really good information so they never felt unprepared. They didn't get that in their other lives, whether with other boards or in their workplace. Any board chair who served when I was executive director would tell you, "She made my job so easy." That's a great compliment, and what does that mean? It's everything I pointed out, and it's the foundation of trust.

Thriving Point:

As executive director, earn the trust of your board and board chair by knowing and being the role. Be accurate, reliable, decisive and open. You are and always will be the lighthouse of your organization.

How are you sourcing your board members?

THERE ARE VARYING STYLES and varying opinions on this topic, and they're at odds most of the time. When I was executive director, I had a lead role in identifying potential new board members because I saw my role as a scout, like a scout for a hockey team. I had to be watching the community for who was the best talent for our Mission.

In our sector, the process for sourcing board members is murky. If I asked you who identifies the talent for your board, you might say the board generates its own people and controls itself. And it consults with the executive director on the decision to bring someone on. This is where you get into the breakdown between what is the role of the executive director and the board. There's a reason it's so often lopsided, disjointed and dysfunctional.

Many executive directors and CEOs are not objective. They're not willing to be a scout. They would rather be a taskmaster and a control freak. And that's where the danger shows up, because they can build a board of like minds who feed their ego or their own agenda. That's like building your own Titanic. It's gonna implode.

So, you can see why there's a tug of war over who builds the board. I think an executive director should play a critical role. But in most organizations, that's not how it's done, because the executive director won't take a stand for the Mission and put it ahead of their ego or their drive. They fall down by bringing people in the door for the wrong reasons or with the wrong filter. Friends, colleagues and allies of the executive director are your Titanic.

A similar thing happens if the board goes off and does its own thing and doesn't consult the executive director. The people coming onto the board don't understand the partnership. Added to that, there's no training to get on a board. The training happens after you're on a board.

The reality is that on a typical board, there may be nine to twelve seats. It's not so much who is in the seats; it's about the thinking happening in the seats. When I think about replacing board members, I look at whom I have in the seats. Three are really good at understanding what money is and what money does. Three are really good program thinkers and understand the heart of what we do. And another three are bulldozers, meaning they plow things out and they push for things. Our conversations are so much richer because we aren't all talking the same language.

When you've got varying thinkers around the board table rather than a group of clones, you can put an item on your agenda that says, *What should we be thinking about?* because your board table has varying points of view. They aren't all eating the same grain from the same trough. In a boardroom, that's the catalyst for success.

Thriving Point:

The secret to sourcing new board members is to be the scout seeking various kinds of talent in your community.

Are you bringing the right people onto your board?

Boards behave a lot like people in a canoe. A canoe doesn't move on its own; only when you put the paddle in the water and push. You might say to someone, "Hey, you want to go canoeing?" And many will strap themselves safely into a life jacket, sit in the canoe with their sunglasses on, and bask in the day. But a canoe is hard work; it only moves when someone is willing to take the paddle and put in the muscle. It doesn't matter who you canoe with. There will always be one or two who just want to sit there and drift along. Exactly like a board.

Many people join a board thinking, "This is nice. This is comfortable. I like this work. It feels good to be on this board." Actually, every month an organization is alive, it's whitewater, and if you think you can take a canoe through whitewater, you're crazy. That's where it falls apart. The comfort of being at the board table is smashed when the rapids hit. Someone is going overboard. It could be the executive director; it could be the board chair. Either way, something is going to change. And that's a constant in a nonprofit with a board. Too many think of the board table as a canoe out for a lazy paddle. As an executive director, your job is to look for those special people who will take the paddle and steer, saying, "We're gonna pull this through, whatever it takes."

Keep in mind, there are board chairs who like to sit in the comfort zone and let someone else do the heavy work. That's when organizations stagnate; they float along and forget why they're there. They have all the reasons why they can't do this or that. But they're still at the table, still in the canoe. You've got to figure out who's at that table (who's in that canoe), because you can sink it.

As a brand new executive director, I realized I could move people into and out of the board in the first 100 days, a period when so many board members tend to resign. And I thought, "If you can resign, can you be invited to leave?" That was the question. To resign is *your* action. What if *I* want action? What does that process look like?

And then I started asking questions. What happens if you get someone on a board who is not adding value, not contributing, isn't a team player, or isn't doing what's best for the organization? I'd ask other executive director colleagues, "What do you do when you have someone like this on your board?" And they said, "Reach for your bylaws. Reach for your policy."

What every organization has in its favour is a set of guiding bylaws. One of those is *term*. Nowadays at least, no one becomes a board member for life. They become a board member for a specific term, a set period of time. And increasingly there are only a certain number of terms allowed before they exit the board. I remember speaking to someone who had a board member that served for 21 years, and they were complaining about them. No wonder. They'd been on the board longer than they'd been married to someone — not doing anything and hanging onto customs, practices and events from the distant, no-longer-relevant past.

Something to keep in mind is the value of history and memory. If you have all board members who just joined last year, you have today and the future. But you also need someone with some memory around the organizational depth that adds value to the conversation as to why things are as they are today. You need continuity, meaning you don't want everyone coming in at the same point.

It's easy for new board members to throw out the old broom. Except that old broom probably works okay. New board members like to say, "Well, I'm here now, and I think we should get a new broom." It's wise at this point to be able to ask a board member who was there for some history. What can you tell us about this broom? How has it worked in the past? This gives the conversation depth. At the same time, too many voices from the past are just dead weight, and can cause your organization to stand still and reminisce about old times.

So who are the right kind of board members? There are three criteria. People who will speak the truth. People who have some courage and show it. People who are going to listen to others. Hard to find in a single person. Find people who have some of each of those and then you start giving them an opportunity to grow those strengths.

Most executive directors don't think in terms of growing the strengths of their board members. Instead, they create a little cluster of people whom they can rely on because they know them well and they like one another. They see that as a safety net if things go askew. The approach is, "Well, at least one-third of my board are in my court. I can count on them because we do dinners and golfing." Unfortunately, that's how it works in too many organizations.

To successfully manage your board, remember that everyone brings with them something to contend with. As an executive director, the board is your employer, and there's an unwritten rule: you have to "take over" or manage your employer. You don't wake up every day thinking you have to take command; rather, you have to be willing and able to take command whenever the need arises. It comes at you from unexpected directions, and you never know when you have to bring that command out.

At one point as executive director, I had a board member who served for a few years back in the early 2000s, and she was invited back to serve her second term on the same board fifteen years later. When she was on the board previously, she was a social worker in government. She had a heart for the Mission, was a decent person and very well respected. She joined the board for this next round as a retired person and brought with her a money issue. She was fixated on it and threatened by the financial stability of the organization because she remembered the money struggle when she served previously.

Now, back on the board again, she would leave a meeting and come to my office. "Do you have more annual reports?" Her friends were asking her question after question about what we were doing with our funds. Apparently, they were really badgering her. The third time this discussion happened in my office, I said to her, "I don't get your friends. They're pounding you out there. You don't need more annual reports. You need new friends. Because you're tying me up with people who are not only consuming you, but also consuming my time with crazy-making. More annual reports are not the solution." That saga ended, but the situation did not change. She still kept the same friends. So the question for an executive director is, who is in command of the board? Are you going to feed the monster, or slay it?

Thriving Point:

Figure out your board early and quickly, and set a process in place for getting the right people into the room.

Compelling
and
Practical
Fundraising

Fundraising: whose job is it?

Have you ever wondered why your organization struggles year after year with fundraising? Are you prepared for the real answer to this question? Because the truth could be very uncomfortable for you.

When I first entered the nonprofit world, what I learned was that a good executive director hires a director of development. Then they put that person "over there", and fundraising is that person's job. I've watched organizations where that model is in place…and it wasn't working. Yet a point of pride was, "We have a fundraising staff." They were blessed and relieved. The attitude was, "I checked that off, I don't have to think about it, I give them a budget to meet, and I don't know what happens after that." Everywhere I went and everyone I listened to said the model was like this. And I thought, "No, I'm going to learn to fundraise."

So I was executive director first and fundraiser second. I decided to jump into it in a big way and figure out how to do it. I was looking for techniques, and I found many people out there who work solely on fundraising. All the while, I saw all these executive directors saying it's not their job. But because I was doing both roles, I thought, "One doesn't exist without the other." So I started talking to my staff and board, and I said, "We all have a share in this. We each have a stake in this. If it's gonna happen, we have to be the ones to do it."

By and large, everyone else is doing the model of executive director hires a director of development. That's fine, but it doesn't release the executive director from the role and the prime responsibility that comes with that position, and I personally never had a director of development. I had people who assisted with fundraising, but I led it. And that's a capacity thing. We never had the staffing model with the resources to create a full-time position. By default, I taught everyone else how to fundraise. Funny enough, that is the model that has worked.

The most insidious thing that happens on boards occurs when the executive director tells the board, "We've hired a director of development." And the board folds their arms and says, "Great! They'll raise some money." It takes the pressure off the board, and it lets the executive director say to the board, "I didn't want to do that. Now we have a professional dedicated solely to that. Thank God." So instead of a director of development coming in as a tool and a resource to train, teach and inspire a board, they see it as delegating fundraising "over there" and washing their hands of the responsibility.

And that is so true today. I see it everywhere, and it's not a mystery why most fundraisers don't stay very long in their positions. I suspect that most fundraisers, executive directors and boards only know about asking for support. They never ask themselves, "Who am I in this?" In the absence of that, it's only a *half ask*. Because they're not really *in* it.

As executive director, I always cultivated a mindset around giving. I firmly believe fundraising is everybody's job, and it's a mindset of *asking vs. giving*. The *giving* mindset is, "I need to influence you and have you participate." So if I have you do the ask, you have to be willing to ask the question, "Will you give money?" And you have to really believe in the cause, the work or the Mission. You have to *own* it. You have to *be* the work. You can't half ask. If you do, they're going to feel it. Your very being has to tell them, "I know you're going to want to give $100 because this is what we're going to do." And just from your approach...not just your words, but how you look at them and how you tell a story about what the work is...you'll walk away with a yes.

There are mixed views on whether board members and staff should give. For the board, many feel they give their time. For staff, they feel working for the cause is enough without giving a donation. Yet both board and staff are insiders and they know the cause intimately. It's a simple philosophy: you support that which you believe in. Your presence is a signal that you believe. What we believe in, we support. In nonprofits, that's when the money hits the table.

Here is an incredibly effective way of handling the expectation of fundraising in your organization. When someone comes on the board or on staff, have them sign off on that they will contribute. No need to set a specific level, but have them sign a commitment that they will personally give. With my staff, there was an expectation they would be a monthly donor and give a nominal amount. It was an investment and a statement of giving because they wanted to. It wasn't required, but it was urged. Then I gave them a menu so they could self-identify where and at what level they were going to give.

A super-memorable fundraising program that I led had 27 revenue streams. Many were just tiny slivers of revenue, but they were all important. And there was a slice for everyone. You could drop coins in a box, give monthly, exhaust yourself at events, or give one generous donation a year. Joining the board or joining the staff, you were immersed in the fundraising wheel and how it turned.

As executive director, I always said that it's everyone's job to give, and it's everyone's job to ask. Taking it a step further, it's also everyone's job to protect the asset. I told them, "What is here and what is used here came from the people who gave the money to do it. It starts with turning off the lights when you leave a room. It continues with checking flyers and sales when you go shopping for food for the organization. Use the money wisely. Look after it. Put the basketballs away in the storage bin rather than leaving them all over the yard overnight where they could disappear. When you consciously decide how the money is spent, you'll always have money."

Most people have never bumped into the concept, "Let's protect what we have so we don't waste." It may have been drilled into them when they were raised as children, but I don't know that they ever saw themselves in it. Of course, it's critical in a nonprofit because it stretches the dollar that much further. The better everyone looks after things, the more money there is to do different things. If you're constantly buying glue because people don't put the cover back on, you aren't protecting what you've been given. There is only so much money in the bucket.

I taught giving, asking, and protecting. Behaviour says everything. And that has worked very well for people who may be at a point in life where they can't give a lot of money. Some people for whatever reason can't put cash into it, but when they hear how they can have a hand in using the resources available, they excel. They really get it, and they self-regulate. When they see someone wasting and not protecting, they're right on it. It's hard work to do it like this, but it's one important way to represent your brand as a careful and frugal user of community resources.

Thriving Point:

How do you end up with an organization that has to chase money? You start with an entire staff and board that decided fundraising isn't their job. That's how. It's everyone's job to raise money.

Where do your fundraising ideas come from?

WITHOUT A DOUBT, what made the organization successful where I served as executive director was my ability and willingness to keep my eyes wide open as I looked out in the world for great ideas. Surprisingly however, although there are great ideas to be found in the nonprofit world, my very best ideas were found elsewhere.

Many of our organization's strengths came because I looked beyond our backyard and thought, "That's a great idea. I'm going to tweak it and turn it into something that will fit our market." And true success came when I scaled those ideas in a way most wouldn't consider, which is that I scaled them to be smaller.

My first attempt at "going small" happened in my early days as an executive director. I was a huge fan of *The Price Is Right* game show, and an even bigger fan of Bob Barker as the host. So one day, I declared it was time for us to put on a *The Price is Right* show. Looking back, my enthusiasm was probably the oxygen others needed to buy in when logic was saying, "You've gotta be crazy!" Because they got on board with it.

Along with a committee of six volunteers, we put the show together. As a group, we watched *The Price is Right* three times and noted the games and prizes we liked. We gathered $15,000 worth of prizes, including a living room set and bedroom set. And then there was the issue of Bob Barker. We needed someone cool, lean, not too tall, and older who would emcee the event. You can't have the *The Price Is Right* without Bob Barker, right? Nobody would believe us. So we found our Bob Barker, and we launched it in November for one night. We sold advance tickets and we had over 500 people in the room. It was a bizarre idea at the time, but it had real community appeal.

The next time I scaled a project was when I was rolling out a big fundraiser. I'd seen the Dream Home Lottery in other states and provinces for several years, and it had never left my mind. In 1993, I landed in Edmonton, Alberta. I knew they had been successfully producing the large scale, Million-Dollar Dream Home for communities with a million people.

Once I looked into the Million-Dollar Dream Home model, I knew I wanted to take it back home and scale it down to fit my community. I wanted to miniaturize it. We don't have a million people, but my gut told me we had enough to support this model if it was scaled down to a small population.

The Dream Home Lottery was dealing in large urban areas and selling tickets. I said, "Let's put that into this community and call it Dream Cottage." Everyone got really excited. At the time, it was a "way out there" idea. Here we are 28 years later, and the Dream Cottage is one of the most successful fundraisers do we do each year. Yes, it's a lottery — one that has provided sustained funding, hundreds of long-term supporters, and an amazing conversion rate of individuals to other donor and fundraising opportunities.

Thriving Point:

Resist the urge to always go big, particularly when there's an even greater opportunity to go small.

When do you bring a fundraising project to a close?

CONSIDER HOW LONG you hang onto fundraising projects before you let them go. Time and again, I see organizations running outdated projects that have zero life left in them. They're barely hanging on. The organization is squeezing every last drop out of a fundraiser the public no longer supports or cares about, and does that for years on end. It's an epidemic.

I took the opposite approach in the organization where I was executive director. On my window in my office, I had a beautiful piece of stained-glass artwork. It was three feet high and 20 inches wide and the scene was Noah's Ark. I chose to put it in a window with suction cups where the temperature changes to the extreme four times a year: it was inevitably going to break. Once when I returned from a trip, one of my staff said, "I'm so glad that didn't fall off the window and break while you were gone." I said to her, "It's going to." I'm sure she thought I was callous.

The truth is, I put it up there because I wanted the beauty of it, even though I knew it was going to break. It's a way of thinking, of stepping into reality and understanding this is how it is. As a young child, I watched my home burn. That was tragic, and I lost my favourite things. I also learned that when it happens, you start over. You have to be willing to release your attachments and create what's next.

One of my first experiences with this was a very successful fundraising project we called Bowl for Kids.

The concept was team-based bowling. We gathered teams of five people from a business, an organization or a municipal council. Those five-person teams with pledge sheets in hand went out and solicited their friends, neighbours, family and coworkers to raise money. And they brought it to the event. And then of course, we used it to fulfill our Mission.

Bowl For Kids grew to be community wide. Every business, every bank, every government office had a team involved. So instead of five people out there trying to raise money for Big Brothers Big Sisters, we had around 125 teams of five people each. Our total feet on the ground grew exponentially, and they were asking on our behalf. It was *the* fundraiser at the time. We scaled it up to the point where we were raising around $75,000 in one event. Per capita, we had the highest dollar average per person for any community. Huge results!

But nothing is forever. The first clue that we needed to shut down Bowl For Kids was an economic indicator. Like every community, things were shifting. In planning for the upcoming event, which was still a year out, I looked at all the photos of teams who had participated over the years. I was really surprised when I put an X by the 19 teams where the businesses had closed. There was a dramatic downward dip in our community, and I thought, "There will be no team from all these places." I knew our results would be down because we didn't have the employment levels where people are going to rally around the project. That was a real wake-up call for me. Also, what struck me was, "If I'm only going into a bowling center once a year myself, how many other people are only going once a year? And how long is this behaviour going to continue?" They may love it, but they don't come back and do it the next month for fun. So I realized that we had an activity that is losing relevance… and I knew we had to change things up.

The other thing that changed during the course of the Bowl For Kids run was that we had gone online with it. Doing so automatically reduced the level of engagement. Until that point, a person would have to go up to their buddy and ask for sponsorship. It wasn't just a transaction; it was a relationship and a one-on-one connection. We also looked at the product — bowling. People don't bowl anymore. The numbers were still good, but I looked around and realized that the only time people bowled was when we held Bowl for Kids. I saw an aging population and a lot of seniors, the variables that would eventually affect it. And as bowling became less popular, the facilities closed. And so I thought, "We've got some real threats here to this project, and we need to look into our future. But what's life without bowling?"

That said, Bowl for Kids gave us our foundation to do everything else, because we did it for so long over 20 years. It engaged so many people. We could still go into offices and homes and see pictures of people's bowling teams. Even today, when people in our community pass on, they often mention in their obituaries having supported Big Brothers Big Sisters and Bowl For Kids. It had real value in people's lives. It was so personal, and they were so connected. So it was our springboard.

Other Big Brothers Big Sisters agencies are still rolling those balls, and every year the revenue keeps dropping. With blinders on, they ignore the reality of the activity and fear what's going to replace it. Meanwhile, it's draining away and they don't look around because they have their heads down doing what they've always done.

As executive director, I always had to be thinking—what's going on here that I may not even feel or see yet? I woke up looking for it, and I was also very patient. I didn't have a knee-jerk reaction and press the panic button. I wanted a certain level of understanding before going in a particular direction.

Thriving Point:

Step into reality and recognize that whatever "it" is, it's going to expire, leave, stop, run its course, and not last forever, because everything has an end.

What makes a person say yes to your *ask*?

I HAVEN'T SPENT MUCH TIME thinking about asks, and never really wondered what was the "right" way to ask. When I was learning the ropes, I was likely vague, timid, and shy, so I didn't get the answers I needed. The question wasn't clear, so I learned to ask it so that when a person heard it, they knew exactly what was being asked of them.

Once as an executive director I made an ask to a potential board member. She was busy and involved. I looked at her profile and thought, What's the likelihood of her saying yes? And I didn't know the answer. So I made a cold call and told her why I was calling. I said, "The organization needs you and I want to talk with you in person and explain what that means." So she already knew going into that meeting that I was going to ask her to be a board member.

When she came into the meeting, I knew her so there wasn't a lot of setup. We were familiar with one another. I knew going in I was going to start with why I was asking then, followed by what I was asking for, followed by why I hadn't asked before then. Those were my three angles.

I zeroed right in on what the need was, and what would be a good match with her interests, her personality, and her skills. And then I presented what I wanted to do with her on the board and why I hadn't asked until then. She'd had a rough patch in her life where she would want to be low-profile, so I said, "We had to take time to bring you in…not only for you personally, but also from a public perception standpoint. The time is now."

She said yes.

A typical ask can be something more mundane. So if we needed a canoe, I would look for someone who could likely provide one. Perhaps an outfitter in the community. And I would tell them within five minutes why I was there. I let them know who I was representing and would say, "This is what we're doing with 17 or 18 young people. We need a canoe for an event for about eight hours. I know you've got a canoe business, and we'll pick it up and return it when we're done. Do you think this is possible? Can you give it to us? Do you expect a fee? What do we need to do to make this work?"

I offered options. Free was first, but then I acknowledged it's not always free. In the early phases of the organization, when cash reserves were nonexistent, free was very common. The case didn't change much though. I always made sure that whomever I asked wasn't confused. I didn't snow them with information that wasn't relevant to the ask. It was quick and clean.

What I see in how other people ask is that it's sometimes very slick and polished, but it's vague and misleading. In fact, it's often confusing. People are so murky with their requests that I often don't even know they've made one. And they walk away empty-handed because while they thought they asked, all they really did was confuse. People don't respond to statements. They respond to requests. Murky asks show up in two places — written and oral, but especially in verbose and wordy oral efforts. I see people go off in all directions, trying to explain all sorts of things, postponing and in the end failing to make a simple direct ask.

The buzz word and strategy of fundraising for organizations is major gifts. So in essence, there's the art of the major gift ask, and it's the same formula everywhere. You are looking for people with the capacity to give. You filter your screen, research them, and Google them inside and out. You ask yourself, "What can I find out before we meet?" You try to get someone to introduce you. Finally you're there in person with them, and you take along a buddy, a board member or senior volunteer who has an affiliation or an attachment to them. And you spend that first half-hour asking probing questions to hear their story. The obvious strategy is to zero in on their interests.

The truth is that people who have money are busy. If you're going to get them to give some of what they have away, you have to be direct, because that's usually how they deal. They don't want to have tea and go up and down and around the mountains with stories. That'll come perhaps, but it is *not* an ideal strategy. Unfortunately, however, that is the whole "art" of major gift asks…and it's *so* contrived.

When you make an ask of someone who has resources or finances you want to access, the more direct and simple the ask, the more success you're going to have. That said, you had better know how often your organization has dealt with this person. Because with the rampant turnover of people in the sector, you don't want to go unaware through a door that has been knocked on many times before you. They'll remember. They will remember the organization, and they will know if you have failed to do your prep work. They'll take that as an reflection of the competence of your organization, and the likelihood of leaving the meeting with a yes is very low.

Many small shops become consumed with how great the work is and how big the need is, and they assume everybody knows and everybody cares the same way.

Wrong! They think because they believe in the cause, it will happen. That's a huge assumption, and it stems from unpreparedness and inexperience. "We do good work and therefore you should want to help us." No, that's not how it works.

The organization where I served as executive director created a charitable foundation for future work that ignited a stream of asks for money from other organizations and individuals. I discovered three things that characterized every ask. No exceptions.

1. They came in with one skimpy list, a one-page document with little or no appropriate information or material.

2. They were not ready. When I asked them a question, they looked at each other with "I don't know" written all over their faces. The questions I asked were questions that anyone representing the organization should know.

3. I always asked them to provide something to me in a follow-up email…something simple such as an annual report or something else. I never once received a follow-up email after an ask.

The most recent ask that walked into my office when I was executive director was typical. Sloppy work is rampant, and this was a great example. They walked in with a poorly-constructed ask, and obviously had put no thought into their strategy. They hadn't decided on their roles or discussed who would lead. They didn't share the presentation (if that's what you would call it), and it was obvious that they hooked up in a parking lot and arrived in my office not long after.

They asked for a significant amount…six figures, and gave me one option only. They were clearly focused on what they wanted, and didn't have the consideration or courtesy to say, "You may want to consider supporting this way, or this way, or this way." I would've expected to see different levels or ranges. None of that. They made an assumption based on our capacity, and they came in at the highest need they had. Sloppy.

The paper they provided me was skimpy and flimsy, without their names or the name of the organization. It was a poorly-printed Excel spreadsheet, so I thought, "If I were to take this and sit with another decision-maker in our organization, or a colleague, or a board member, I would be embarrassed to put this in front of them." So I said, "If you could email me a good copy of this, I will review it." I never got it, and never heard from them again. They dropped the ball.

On another occasion, two women come to me from a school. I knew them both and they're great people. They came to see if we would fund a half million for their playground. The first thing the leader said was, "I know you probably don't want to do the half million for our playground, but I thought we'd ask." It was like a kid who's 14 asking to go out: "I know you're not gonna let me, but it's Saturday night and it's with my friends, but I know you're not gonna let me." She had already decided for me. Another sloppy ask.

Yet another interesting example was with a really successful youth orchestra in my province. It's a strong organization with a good following and the organization I led had supported it with $20,000 a year for the previous four years. The chief fundraiser for the orchestra called me and said, "I have posters for our concert in October.

Would you like to be a ticket outlet for us? I'm right in town and I could stop by and drop these off." I said "Sure".

Then he said, "Well, we are putting together our sponsorships. Would the Boys & Girls Club consider being a sponsor for our event for $500? You get your name in our program, and it'll be announced from the stage. Would that fit in your budget?" I said, "No, I'm not interested in the $500 sponsorship. But yes, we'll take posters and we'll be a ticket outlet for you." He said, "Oh that's fine. I've got posters and if I have a chance, I'll drop by." He never came by, and lost an opportunity to strengthen his relationship with a long-term supporter.

Keep in mind, back then we had a four-year donor commitment with the orchestra. We were up for renewal and he was not a rookie when it came to the ask. The decision to continue sponsorship was an item in a board meeting. The takeaway I had was *ouch*. It feels really different when you've been a contributor and that's how you're treated. It was mindless, and you don't get to be mindless. People remember for a long time.

Sadly, many nonprofits are similarly afflicted. Working from scarcity and desperation, with a near-total disregard for who they're asking, they fail to play through in their head what their careless asks sound like or where they land. They pick up the phone or turn the doorknob without thinking the process through carefully, and *boom*.

Still other organizations whine for their needs instead of choosing to highlight their successes and share some inspiration around, "the work we do matters." They talk about their bucket and how many leaks it has in it, instead of how full their bucket is. That's a turnoff. When I got calls, they were primarily focused on the struggle.

If I spoke to a colleague, it was all about the struggle. Don't forget: *everyone* struggles.

Thriving Point:

The key to a powerful ask is being direct in your request and crafting an ask that makes it easy to say yes.

What kind of money are you seeking in your organization?

THERE'S A CHRONIC FUNDRAISING "PUSH", a rampant struggle, primarily due to the upheaval in staffing. For decades the challenge has been that most people leave fundraising jobs before two years is up. That's a lot of churn; they're out the door and starting over.

Meanwhile, donors and supporters are left answering yet another cold call or meeting with another new face…or perhaps they are forgotten entirely. This treadmill shows no signs of slowing down, because the staff turnover in nonprofits is directly tied to many issues beyond their control. So the fundraisers, stymied in their desire to grow where they are, make the one move they can control, which is out the door. And if you're looking for significant gifts, it's really bad news, because research shows that if you're going to master major gift fundraising, you need to stay at least seven years. That's how long it takes to build a relationship with an individual who is going to give you massive money.

Let's say the fundraiser's name is Charlie. He wants to inspire someone at the million-dollar giving level because of their success in life, and he starts to build a relationship. Perhaps he makes a visit, email, or call and starts to get to know that person. Then, with the process barely under way, he makes a sudden exit. Unfortunately, as soon as that potential donor calls and Charlie is gone, the organization is back to square one. So if Charlie doesn't stick around as a fundraiser for ten to twelve years, it drops an awful lot of relationship threads. The million dollars never comes, and the struggle continues.

There are two approaches, and this is one: the charity or nonprofit that believes all the focus should be on the home run, the major gift. So they're not looking to speak to John, Jane and Jerry on the street. They're looking for those three or four people in their city who have deep wealth and trying to get in front of them. The money is out there; all the big institutions need to get it; the competition is fierce; and the odds are long.

And then there are all of those nonprofits who are getting what I call "micro money," like $2 at the cash register for a cause … and what I call the "middle money" that is ignored by so many fundraisers, somewhere between $100 and $500 a year. I personally support three charities that I really like and I'm in the middle-money category for all three of them.

Anyone can get $2 from you if they corner you or approach you the right way. It's a transaction. You give, you blink, you're gone…and a lot of money is raised that way. But what about getting $300 from you in the next year? If I talked to you and discovered what you were interested in, I bet I could convince you to give $25 a month. And if the organization did their job well and shared the story of what that money was doing, it wouldn't be hard to get that money again. And again. At that level, if the system is in place (even though Charlie had left), I'd continue to give $25 a month, provided I was being made aware of what my money was doing. And it would be even better if I heard from you now and then…other than when you want me to give you money.

Thriving Point:

Take a good look at where you've decided to chase a certain kind of money to fund your Mission...and what you're giving up as a result.

What is your fundraising mentality?

Most nonprofits I am exposed to are staring at the budget when deciding on their next fundraiser, hoping to win and terrified to lose. Many expect a winner right out of the gate despite the fact that history has always shown otherwise. In my 30 years as executive director, I've noticed that most conversations within most organizations are based on scarcity. Our industry language tends to be sourced from stress, worry and regret, particularly where fundraising is concerned. And I can relate.

Despite successfully raising the money needed to keep the doors open, at one point as an organization we found ourselves in a negative cycle, in terms of both language and outlook. Once we recognized it, we chose to do something about it, and one year our staff and board chose together to deliberately change our language from "needs" to "dreams." Specifically, we consciously committed to what I now call the *one-two punch* in nonprofit conversation: What if?

An interesting thing happens when you ask, "What if?" By beginning with those two simple little words, you naturally create immediate, unresisted expansion. In fact, our agreed-upon rules around this were, "no one is wrong" and "there are no boundaries." With these common understandings in place, we began with a blank page and asked, "What would we like to do in the next calendar year?" This was especially useful the year we bought and moved into our new building.

Upon moving in, I asked myself an important question, "How are we going to get traffic to our door and get people inside?" I needed an event that generates exposure and brings people through the door who ordinarily wouldn't come. I knew there were many people who wouldn't be involved at any level or participate in any of our fundraisers—but for the right event, they'd *want* to come. That's when I created the Festival of Trees.

The model was decorated Christmas trees that are auctioned off and taken home, a model that has been used in many places. We bought 30 artificial trees, and each was connected to a business. If you had a business and you sponsored a tree, your name was at the bottom. Every tree had a different theme, and it was the sponsor's job to decorate their tree. This connected us with the business community, which was great, but the public just wanted to see beautiful trees. Aside from the Christmas trees, we had a whole table up through the center of the hall loaded with lower-priced Christmas items such as wreaths and centerpieces. You could bid on about 200 items to take home as gifts.

Our core volunteers, the ones who knew the Mission inside and out, were at the door when people came in and when they left. We gave visitors a little takeaway, a booklet with our story. It was a ton of work, and our commitment to quality made it an exceptional five-star event. When we launched it, I focused on including the right volunteers. After all, this was the first time the public was going to be able to walk into our building. In fact, for most, it was the first time they had heard of us!

We ran the Festival of Trees from the last day of November through the first four days of December: ample time for people to get into the Christmas spirit, and soon enough to take their Christmas tree home and enjoy it for the next three weeks. The event was an over-the-top success because it brought people in and showcased our facility, and we got to have face-to-face conversations. We achieved our primary goal: for people who had never before had any connection with us to know where we were and learn about what we did. We ran it for 15 years, and we made some money, but for us it was truly and by design a *Friendraiser*. It brought people to us in a very tangibly positive experience.

When we retired the Festival of Trees, we gifted the event to Hospice, another charity that was struggling to gain awareness and traction in the community, and since then they've carried the torch. In a similar vein, we've passed on several other successful fundraising projects to still other groups in the community. We passed Travelotto to the Rotary Club, and the Duck Race (which ultimately got away on us) we shared with Camp Sheldrake. Seeing those projects get recreated to fit the needs of other deserving local organizations were gratifying community milestones for us.

We didn't realize its true value and how deep it had taken us with our connection to the community until we wrapped up our final Festival of Trees campaign. People started calling us and asking about it. We are still often asked about it. Over and over people say, "That's how I started my Christmas every year." Connecting people to our Mission through our events has been a wellspring of deep, long-lasting community relationships.

Thriving Point:

Ditch the "quick fix" and "overnight success" mentality which doesn't exist. Instead, ask yourself, "How does it fit in the market I'm in? Will we get a new supporter? And how will it tie to the work we're doing with our Mission here?"

What is your approach to fundraising?

IF I HAD THE CHANCE to observe one of your fundraising projects from start to finish, I could predict with reasonable accuracy the future of your organization. Will you merely survive or thrive? How you approach a fundraising project would give me that answer.

So what is the difference between me and you? Quite simply, I'm fully aware that when I start a fundraising project, it can fail. Most people have a fear of failure. I, however, expect to fail and I know I'm gonna learn, and it doesn't hold me back. I try it. If it fails, I'm going to the next one. I know there is another failure coming. That's the approach I've always taken. I have several failures in my past, and here is one of them…

Like so many nonprofits do, we did a duck race fundraising project. Very simply, people bought a ticket with a number, and there was a duck with that number printed on the bottom. We presold all the tickets for $5 per duck and the race was on a particular day. Duck races are always done in open, flowing water.

We did the duck race masterfully for three years. We had the perfect conditions for this event. We had a beautiful river that was the perfect setting, and people loved it. It was a family thing. We had really good momentum. I thought, "This has a long life."

The one challenge was that our river was tidal. So we had to figure what time of day to hold the race and which way the river was going. It's minor in some respects, but important. In the fourth year, with 12,000 ducks in the race, we made some poor choices as to who was to be out on the water letting the boom go, and they didn't handle it properly.

They pulled the trigger too soon and let the boom go. The ducks spread far and wide all over the river, making it impossible to catch the first duck at the finish line. In fact, there was no finish line. It was pure free-float for thousands of ducks. As supporters, fans and duck-owners stood on the shore trying to see where "their duck" went, it was clear to us the race was over…in more ways than one. We couldn't declare a solid, true winner that day, and many people trudged home unhappy.

The duck race was our first public fundraising failure. We took a lot of pain at the event itself and a beating in the media on how poorly it was done. The board got together afterward and did an autopsy of the event. The ending was abrupt and unpleasant. So what did I do? I did what I always do: I went on to the next one…

We were looking to do a fundraiser that wasn't being done anywhere. In my community, there is a fresh lobster season, so we decided to host a lobster dinner. And we thought, "Who loves lobster? A lot of guys do." So we targeted this event for Father's Day.

We did a massive outreach. The Mission of Big Brothers Big Sisters was kids who at that time didn't have a dad or a role model. The community didn't have many other fundraising events on Father's Day, so we were excited at the idea of hosting a dinner. We sourced and purchased lobster. It was June, the opening of the season. The lobsters were super-expensive and we had to cook them because they were live. We bought 2,000, priced the dinner and booked the hall, which could seat 200 at a time.

We started the lobster dinner at 2:00 p.m. that day, and agonized for three hours watching as no one came. The end result? We sold 89 dinners out of 2,000 lobsters. We owned the lobsters though, and there was no going back. Initially it was a tragic disaster. We had all this food that was going to perish. Most of the volunteers in the room that day were men. It was their day too, and here we had just crashed what was going to be an amazing event.

I looked around the hall and thought, "I need to identify two men here who are well known and likeable, and who will take two half-ton trucks, go into the community and sell the lobster so we don't bleed this project." I found those two guys and said, "It's 5:30. We only have three hours to turn these lobsters into money and cover our cost." They spent an hour loading two vehicles. We got a cardboard sign and set it on the side of the road. And those two guys sold out all our lobsters by 8:00 p.m. that night.

Let's face it, most people would have put the lobsters in the freezer and waited until the next day to sell a few lobsters at a time. Most would likely have gone to waste. And everyone would have had an opinion of how to get rid of them, to say nothing of how the event should have been properly handled. We would have owned an unmitigated, dragged-out community disaster. But in the end, we managed to pull it out of the fire in a few hours and at least walk away more or less intact.

That was my second year as an executive director. We were clueless and we did some really stupid things that we remember with bittersweet fondness. Another failure? You bet. We misread the market. People love lobster... in their backyard on a picnic table. In our community (and probably many others), Father's Day is not an event where dads get dressed up and go out for dinner. That's Mother's Day. We thought the product would be a pull. Boy did we ever read it wrong!

Thriving Point:

Fundraising is not about getting it right. You must be willing to play the *game* of fundraising. It's about being willing to lose. You have to play the fundraising game to win *or* lose.

What are you willing to do to save your organization?

THIS IS A STORY of redemption, which I remember as if it were yesterday, and it's important to share. Every nonprofit leader has either felt or lived this. Most nonprofits don't keep their doors open when failure is imminent, and if you are facing this reality, I share my story to give you some grit…with a side of hope.

When I was executive director, our Dream Cottage Lottery fundraising initiative launched in 1993. Six successful years later, I said to the board, "We've given away six dream cottages. Every winner sold it because they wanted the cash." I had looked more closely at the buyers. I realized the dream cottage was a burden to some people and they weren't buying tickets because of fear of winning a burden. Not everyone wants a cottage they would have to move to a vacant piece of land.

I proposed doing a cash lottery to replace the Dream Cottage Lottery in 2000. This way, we didn't actually have to buy a dream cottage. We structured it to be very attractive, had a great marketing plan, and rolled it out on the same timeline … without the *physical* dream cottage. So we rolled the Dream Cottage Lottery into a cash lottery. The lottery prize package was all cash draws. A perfect solution given that winners of the cottage converted it to cash.

I told myself it would bring in the non-buyer who saw the prospect of a Dream Cottage as a burden.

The cash option failed ***miserably***. Logic told me that if everyone is playing the lottery to win money, then we should offer money. What I failed to realize is that the dream cottage was the tangible tactile place where people went to get the *dream* and buy a ticket. You don't visualize cash and you can't see what cash can do. You can think about things you want to buy with it, but even then, it's hard to picture it.

We offered cash and failed. Nobody bought tickets. We launched in April. The draw would have been in August or September of 2000, and we knew by June that we were going down. You can only imagine the chuckling of my fundraising friends who had such disdain for lotteries. As executive director, I found myself in the boardroom answering to a board that expected this fundraising disaster would be the crash of our organization. We had lost somewhere between $100,000 and $200,000, and there was no money to stay open for even 30 more days.

It was absolutely horrible. Anyone who has been through a similar experience knows that it bears no comparison to simply being let go from your job or even "going out of business." In our nonprofit world, the impact is usually much greater. When a nonprofit faces the real possibility of closing its doors, you are witnessing an entire ecosystem, a living, breathing organization with a Mission to serve, one that you literally helped create, about to disappear permanently. In our case, an emergency board meeting was scheduled to deal with three specific issues: cutting staff, closing programs and informing the community.

Interestingly enough, in the days leading up to that meeting I was feeling anxious. Not anxious in a negative or somber way, but entirely the opposite...energized. I had a fire in my belly to not only keep our organization alive, but to make it positively flourish. Despite what seemed like insurmountable circumstances, as far as I was concerned there was no way this ship was going down on my watch.

Just before the board meeting took place, I was powerfully pulled to do something. I reached out to a significant donor of the organization and asked to meet with him to share the imminent decisions. I told him what was about to come down, and then did something most people would probably deem insane. I let the donor know I was personally giving $5,000 to keep us afloat. And then I went a step further. On the spot, I asked the donor to match my pledge and give $5,000 of his own money. Without any hesitation he agreed to match the money. That exchange took exactly ten minutes.

At the board meeting, after much agonizing discussion mixed with long stretches of uncomfortable silence, I stood up and announced I was personally giving $5,000 to help us stay afloat. To a table-full of stunned faces I then told them that one of our donors had already agreed to match my $5,000. At that point I said to all the board members present, "I put my commitment on the table. Who else will match our money so we can stay open?" Seven of the ten members immediately said, "I will", and each of them gave $5,000 on the spot. One member gave $35,000.

The end result? I left what was initially planned as a "close out" meeting with $80,000 on the table and our organization's doors not closed, but open. Wide open.

With renewed energy, I declared a comeback in 2001. I said, "We're going back to the product that worked: the Dream Cottage Lottery. We're gonna jump off the bridge, hold our nose and believe that we can give away a dream cottage again with a cash prize option. And this time, we're taking on the burden of selling the dream cottage when the winner takes the cash option." The community responded in spades, and that was the first and only time we sold every single Dream Cottage Lottery ticket. It's never happened that way again, but the organization still runs the Dream Cottage Lottery today, 28 years later, and they sell 85-90% of the tickets every year.

Thriving Point:

Even at your lowest point, you've got to dig deep and find the solution. And that solution often shows up after a giant failure.

How do you know when it's time to hang up a fundraising effort?

IT'S A FUNNY THING about nonprofits. They'll have a regular event or mail-out. Let's say it's direct mail. They'll mail at the same time of the year, to the same people, asking for the same amount. And they won't put any analysis into "What if we tried that six months earlier, or if we create a new offer at a new price?" Instead it's the same "Will you sign up? Will you give us $20 again?"

This is like something you'd see in a fitness gym. There are people who show up and do the same routine every week and wonder why they aren't getting any results. They get different wrinkles and the hair starts to change colour, but the body stays mostly the same. No one would ever know they've been going to the gym so faithfully.

Nonprofits are experts at doing the same thing at the same time each year, getting the same results, and talking about it in the same way. And then they flip the calendar and do it again. It takes a lot of work to keep things the same, to do things the same way you've always done them. As soon as a nonprofit catches wind of the possibility of making any changes to what they're already doing, they shut it down, don't have time, and they gotta go now. They go back to protecting the farm. They're the wolf of their own Mission. This is pretty common, and you wouldn't have to knock on too many doors to find this problem: putting all the organization's energy into maintaining status quo.

If your organization belongs to a national group or federation, you likely have a signature event that every local branch does. It usually raises you some money, right? Rarely though, do you look out into the community to see the signals that tell you it's no longer relevant and people no longer care to participate. The exception that proves the rule—one of the few signature fundraising projects that have stood the test of time is Girl Guide Cookies (and even they have reinvented their offering).

Are you willing to do the analysis it takes to say, "Maybe this is worn out; maybe this is over?" You come out every year with the "Run For Whatever", and it's very possible that people are tired of running. Lots of people already have the t-shirt. Of course you can keep putting out the same product over and over. You can continue expecting to raise money, engage people and inspire and excite them. And likely, you never move the needle on raising more money. Or you can have a look to see if perhaps no one wants to do this anymore. It takes courage to give it up.

Thriving Point:

If you are willing to keep your eyes and ears open, the community will tell you when it's time to retire a fundraising strategy.

Powerful
and
Enduring
Organizations

How do you handle the conversation about overhead in your organization?

OVERHEAD IS LIKE AN ANCHOR. If something is labeled overhead, it's "not needed." But since when did administration, insurance, accounting, rent and marketing become frills? Someone decided overhead is a bad word. People announce all kinds of opinions when they see a line item called overhead. Whereas I took overhead items like telephone, computer, and Internet, and I created a budget that says a portion of that Internet line is needed for camps, mentoring, and so on. Because the Mission is not about having a phone line or Internet connection.

Nonprofits have bought into this whole myth about overhead, and everyone wants to keep it under 10%. Really? Do you know of any schools that run without a principal? A town or city without a manager? Research without labs and scientists? Work doesn't get done without people and tools. That's why you need to do your budget differently.

Nonprofits are expected to do things free or low cost, from where they work, to what they pay staff, how they message and beyond. "Oh, don't waste the money." Whereas in the corporate or capital world, the more you invest, the bigger your impact, and the more innovation and growth.

However, most nonprofits deal in human needs, and it's not *always* about the dollars and the knife to keep things trimmed and pared down. It's more often about how great the need is. What are you prepared to do to get more money? It's easy to cut costs or trim your budget, but the *real* work is to go out there and get the money you need, instead of hiding behind, "Oh, our overhead is low." That badge of honour is exactly why staff turnover is epidemic in the sector. Low wages, inadequate training and no resources to get the job done make a triple play that sets the wheels in motion for staff to head out the door. There's a significant hidden cost in that cycle, but meanwhile, take heart — you're proud of your low overhead. That's a myth. Bring in the ghost busters.

It's time to shine the light on shoestring budgets. Your organization was created to solve a problem and add value. Somewhere it was decided that it was best done "on the cheap," but how little you spend is tied directly to how little you achieve. Why is it noble to brag about low overhead while not moving the needle on advancing your Mission? Surprisingly, it's not your donors or supporters who are demanding low overhead. They're giving and supporting the cause. You are choosing to listen to the external noise demanding low overhead, and you march to that drum.

Stop it. It's time to end the starvation cycle. No one is excited to work in or volunteer in an organization that, as Seth Godin says, "is in a race to the bottom." Flip the conversation and put on a new badge of honour. Be proud of overhead that delivers big time on results, retains staff, values volunteers, invests in IT and spends money — as efficiently as possible — to make money. That's what Seth calls "a race to the top." It's not a cakewalk. It takes guts, drive, risk, persistence, skills and generosity. But it sure puts to bed that silly notion of low overhead as the only way to live in the nonprofit sector.

Start with your board. Many nonprofits exist to meet

a social need, so they tend to get the social thinking types on boards—people in education, healthcare, etc. Those voices don't have a lot of business or financial experience because they're employees, and their pay cheques are auto-deposited. However, they often do have lots of program experience, and they know the issues. You'll also need board members skilled in strategy, finance and business. The key is balance, and a mix of both kinds of board members is best.

The conversation with the board must always focus on *effectiveness*. How do you effectively do the work of the Mission on a shoestring budget? Ask the question, "Which is more important—having low overhead or real solutions for the Mission?" You own the conversation about overhead. You decide if you're proud of low overhead and little progress, or if you truly have a dream that you're willing to race to the top for. It's up to you.

Thriving Point:

Overhead is an ongoing battle in organizations that have yet to create a budget driven by outcomes, impact and benefits. Bust the myth of low overhead. Focus on how much you achieve.

How do you keep the Mission front and centre inside a nonprofit?

WITHOUT QUESTION, leading a nonprofit requires keeping the people who do the work — both the staff and the board — from getting caught in the mundane. It's far too easy to forget the "why," and as executive director, I dealt with it by asking front line staff to go tell another staff in the building what it was like to be on the front lines — so they could have a taste of it.

One example was the little girl who was in her third foster home. She had a Big Sister who visited her in school. She said to her Big Sister, "I don't have my doll anymore." The volunteer asked why. The little girl replied, "Well, I'm not in the same home anymore. And they didn't pack the doll you gave me." So that volunteer called Mandy and told her what happened. Mandy went and found the doll and made sure it found its way to the volunteer for the next visit with the little girl. And I told Mandy, "That's why we're doing the Gold Rush project. You know all those volunteers in that room over there peeling coins? Go tell them about the doll."

Another example — one of our volunteers did the check presentation for the Breakfast Program at one of the schools our organization served. I pointed out to that volunteer, "All those kids not only had cereal, but also they had fruit in that photo you took. Please go tell so-and-so about your experience doing that today." Why? Because that was the engine of the work we did.

In far too many organizations the staff are trapped in reports, graphs, numbers and meetings. They don't talk about the little things that people put in their memories that last them a lifetime. The people in your organization who might never hear about the doll being returned to the little girl — or the breakfast program cheque presentation — are the ones who need to hear it most.

I notice a similar trap in boardrooms everywhere. Most organizations measure quorum. I was in boardrooms where we waited and waited for quorum. I asked, "Why are people not making this a priority?" But I knew the answer. It was likely because the meetings were dry as dust, uninspiring, and led by an agenda dealing with whatever happened last year. How do you immediately change the flavour of that board meeting? By putting your program Mission right at the front.

Bring in a voice — the program director, mentoring leader, or whoever. Have them start the meeting with, "This is what we've done since we were last together." Show some powerful images and let them tell the story from the viewpoint of those who benefitted. That sets the tone in the room. You can still argue and debate. There might even still be some angst in the meetings from time to time. But you know that front and center, you began by having everyone's heart triggered to think, "This is important work." Put the Mission at the opening of your agenda, and the focus in the meeting will be on the *why*.

Thriving Point:

To keep the *why* at the center of your nonprofit, always place the front-line Mission work in front of people — ahead of everything else.

How do you tell the story of your organization?

BACK IN THE EARLY DAYS of the organization I led, we struggled to raise money, and our message wasn't landing on people in a way that produced an outcome. One day, one of our board members said, "We need to put a face on what we do. We need to tell our story and show people how and why this is important." This was a tipping point for the organization. We ramped up our messaging and marketing, and we never stopped. Most organizations don't realize that it's the key to nonprofit success: getting the message out using whatever channel it takes, and investing whatever resources are needed to get the job done. And it pays huge dividends.

Most organizations don't invest in marketing. They choose one strategy, tool or channel — and hit it once. It's a cycle of one. Take an ad out and nothing happens. What this approach overlooks is that you need to hear the same message often, in fact many times, before you act. Unfortunately, that first ad won't usually get you a customer. So you make one appeal, and then you sit and wait…and you expect — hope for — some kind of miracle. Then you analyze the zero results, realize it doesn't work, and use that as justification for not doing it again. The standard rhetoric is, "waste of money, nobody replies."

The other issue is that the "face" on your messaging and marketing isn't *relevant*. For a person to want to say yes and participate with you, your message has to be real and relevant for the people you're targeting. Sadly, so much of the messaging and marketing I see in nonprofits is mistakenly about what's needed. It rarely tells a story designed to grab the attention of someone who would love to say yes, if they only understood why it matters to them. That's your job. To tell your story over and over and over again.

It's really very simple to put a face on the work you're doing. I approached one of my staff at the time and asked her to include something new in the monthly e-newsletter. I wanted to include acknowledgments of unsolicited memorial donations we've received through our website. I said, "Let's start promoting the names of the people who are remembered with memorials." I thought a small low-key acknowledgment would yield more donors. It meant getting a simple graphic, adding the names of the memorials and wrapping it into the e-newsletter. It read "Grateful for the memorial donation received in the name of _____." Simple.

The memorial program had been in place for years but was practically dormant, but when we put the message in front of donors, the giving to the program suddenly spiked. We began acknowledging memorial donations in the e-newsletter beginning in June. In less than two months, the unsolicited memorial donations multiplied. In fact, one newsletter included 14 names because so many donations had come in. The interesting thing is the organization had been doing memorials forever in a very low-profile way. All we did differently at that time was to put it in front of people. That made it relevant enough for many others to honour their friends and family in this way.

Thriving Point:

Put a face on it! Tell your story over and over and over again.

What do people remember about your organization?

Keeping the emotion alive is honouring the emotional needs of people, and sharing emotional experiences is even bigger than telling the story. The story is good, and it has to stir the heart. Stories can be dull, plain, and black and white, but add in the emotion and you have a story in colour—and that is what people remember. Once you have an emotional connection with someone, there's an invisible bond. Trust goes way up, compassion goes way up, and blood pressure goes way down. It's why volunteers serve and it's why people give.

I keep the emotion alive in different ways. When somebody drops in to play Gold Rush, for example, we take a minute and say, "Would you take this pamphlet along with you? You'll see lots of great pictures," and then we tell them one quick fact about something we've done lately. Every staff person is trained to do this. It creates an immediate emotional connection between the person visiting and the work we do. And they walk out the door with that fact in their memory bank. Who knows who else they will share that with?

Equally important is connecting board members individually with the emotion of your organization's work. Whenever I meet with a board member, it's usually one-to-one, whether scheduled or spontaneous. Two things happen right off the bat. First, I sit with them at a table that is fairly small, maybe two feet in diameter. So I am never sitting behind a desk. I sit fairly close to them. Second, the table is always deliberately empty. Nothing on it. I want it to represent a space that if something comes up, we can put it on that table and talk about it.

With board members, we do our quick catch up. And then I tell them something that has gone on in the past few days. Most recently, I told a story about what Randy did when he went to the swim meet. I reminded Lindsey that we sponsor all these kids for swimming. One of those kids, Randy, went to his first swim meet and we covered the costs. While he was there, he earned a medal. Another story I told recently is about the school that called and said, "Hey, we hear what you do in these schools. We want the SNAP program, and we can't wait. Would you please see if you can expand to include our school?"

Sharing not just the story, but also the emotion in the story that comes directly from the people who are impacted, shows our board members that our growth is boundless. Because what we are doing is not just being done well, it is being done so well that more people want it. I make it personal and I make it pertinent to the Mission. That makes it a "wow" moment in their day, which is jam-packed like everyone else's.

Finally, the other way we build emotion in our organization is with all the people who win Gold Rush, our weekly 50/50 lottery draw. Over and over we hear, "Wow, this is such an amazing thing for the community." And I know it's because most people who win have a very emotional story as to what they're hoping to do with the money. They win somewhere around $30,000 currently, and it's life-changing, because it's a release on their pressure valve. Some winners pay off debt. Some tuck it away as a nest egg. Others get to buy the one thing on their wish-list they've dreamed of for a long time. They're all grateful. All are emotional. Stories of winners get told over and over, laced with emotion and gratitude.

Thriving Point:

Rather than simply telling stories, share emotional experiences with everyone in your organization.

What is the Number One thing your nonprofit can do to reignite participation from donors and volunteers?

ONE OF THE BIG GAPS with nonprofits is what I call the *busyness disconnect*, and it gets in the way of doing what works. If the polls, the research and the data show anything about donors and volunteers, it's that they only hear from an organization when they need something. It's not a relationship. It's a hit. And they're tired of being *hit* from so many different nonprofits, either for money or time, and never hearing anything else about the organization. This isn't something unique to nonprofits of course, but it's something you need to figure out and fix, because you don't win when your practices aren't for your audience.

For donors, the *busyness disconnect* shows up in little ways. Like they make a donation and they get no receipt and no thank you because "the database isn't working" or "we don't have enough people on staff." The very basic transaction of a nonprofit occurs when someone gives money or time, and you say, "Thank you." But all across the board, that isn't what's happening! The non-response has become the standard way of operating for most nonprofits. You continue it by saying, "we don't have the money," but it's not really that you don't have the money. You've simply decided to work a particular way where you aren't getting the money.

What donors and volunteers are hearing is numbers that they don't understand. Asks for more money. Asks for more time. Needs and problems. What you don't have. Rather than that, what your donors and volunteers really need to hear is what difference is your organization making. What is one little success you've had in a story that leaves them thinking, "Wow, they do really good work," or "Wow, it's a good thing we have them!" And if they hear it and connect to it, they are far more likely to spread the word or give, whether it's money or time. People have to see themselves in something before they go there. It's a hard sell when you sell cold. You can't just dump on people and think they're gonna say yes immediately.

When it comes to volunteers, if you're like most nonprofits, you are pitching things that are not attractive or inspiring. You're not taking the time to narrow it down and get the right people who will do big work for you. You'll find out pretty quickly who is inclined to volunteer. If you just want a stream of noes, ask the wrong people without the right information gleaned from them. You'll get a bucketful of noes, and then you can talk about how there are no volunteers.

If you want different results, however, you need to talk about your organization differently. Your messaging is your problem. People are looking for options, and if you're not getting results, it's because you're not putting options on the table. Have you ever considered that perhaps you don't have anyone getting involved because you're not offering anything they want? Have you considered that you're not making a difference because, just maybe, you haven't told people how easy it is for them to get involved? Instead of inspiring them with how easy it is, you frighten them with how desperate you are and how important it is. That's the tone of the message of most nonprofits. Needy, fearful and scarcity-driven.

Thriving Point:

If you want to revolutionize the results in your organization, transform your messaging.

What is the hidden key for a nonprofit that is known for doing incredible work?

THIS IS THE UNDERLYING THEME of the very best Mission-driven work being done today, both in the organization I led as executive director, and many others.

When it comes to nonprofits, I see three categories, and every nonprofit falls into one of them.

1. The first is what I call "10x" which stands for "10 times," meaning 10x effort. These organizations are working beyond the call to do truly incredible, top-notch work.

2. The second category is the middle layer—credible organizations that are doing good work. They have mastered the difficult process of gathering enough resources and enough people to continue.

3. The third and final category occupies the bottom. These organizations have lost their relevance and exert questionable impact. They are forgotten. No-one bothered to turn off the lights on the way out and say, "Let's fold this shop."

Far too many executive directors and staff will read these criteria and just assume they do not fall into the third category, when in fact they actually do. And an inability to acknowledge that your organization falls into the third category is the reason you're there.

Doing truly *incredible* work inside a nonprofit requires a 10x way of thinking—every day. 10x is rooted in consistency. You can do anything once, but repeat it, and that's where 10x shows up. You're here right now. You're present. But your mind is either a season or a quarter ahead in terms of where you know you're going for sure. And meanwhile you're also moving that back a bit further.

If you have an event on the 30th day of the month, you have it scoped out by the 10th of the month. It's already been delegated who is responsible, and there have been some quick huddles dealing with the potential obstacles and who will knock them down. You don't wait until the 29th of the month or the 12th hour.

If you're an organization known for doing incredible work, 10x thinking shows up in everything you do. Nothing is taken for granted, nor is anything ignored. It shows up when you meet with the board chair and say, "These are the must-do items. Now let's have a difficult conversation about a board member." That's a 10x conversation. It's a willingness to do the heavy lifting that sits right in front of you. All the so-called "small things" are pushed to the level of exceptional.

What I see most often is nonprofits operating in the second and third categories. If you're honest, you know who you are. You're about halfway there. 5x is just enough to hang onto repetition as the way you operate. You do the same things at the same time of year each year. You don't measure anything, so you don't know if you're having any real impact other than how "good" you feel about the work you're doing. You see things that aren't working well, but you don't see ways to fix them. You're content, complacent and accepting the environment you're in. You actually know you could 10x your work, but it would take real effort. And you're just not willing (yet) to dive in at that level.

So let's say I just described you and your organization.

If you're being honest you might be wondering, "I know I'm not giving everything I can. And I actually **do** want to do incredible work. How can I go about stepping up my game to the 10x level?" This is a great question, and it is one I'm happy to answer.

First, take a hard look at everything you've done in the past six months—or choose another time-frame you can easily snapshot. In that six months, what would you **stop** doing if you had a chance? Once you have your answer, answer the question, "**Why** would I stop doing it?" Next, answer the question, "What is it I would like to **start** doing?" And finally, what would you do if you had money? That's the green light everyone is waiting for. Let yourself dream and imagine. Put together a wish-list if it speaks to you.

Now go back a year in your mind. That thing you said you would like to **stop** doing: what was that thing like a year ago? Should you have stopped it then? Why or why not?

There's a reality to face here, which is that you're just repeating the same activities over and over with the same results and without any follow-up analysis. And there has likely never been a point when you questioned whether or not you were doing incredible work. So if you're not, and If you're ever going to do bigger—incredible—work, there are some things you will need to **stop** doing. You need to step off the ledge, and that requires a different level of thinking.

10x thinking showed up in the organization where I was executive director in what probably appeared to be the most trivial ways. We have snow where I live, and many snowstorms. At the time, we hired a new company to do our snow removal. The man doing the work had just acquired a new snowplow. One day outside the building, one of my staff noticed a beautiful, full-sized red snowplow parked right next to our garage, and it was plugged into our building to keep the battery warm. This is rather common where I live.

I asked my staff, "I'm curious, what would you do with that?" She answered, "Nothing." My response? "Well, here's what I'm going to do. I am contacting the company and asking who owns the snowplow, because it was parked on our property overnight without permission. And by keeping it plugged in, he's using the resources of a nonprofit." That's what 10x thinking looks like. I never took the quiet and polite approach when I saw someone wasting our resources. That goes for staff and strangers alike.

It is fundraising, however, where 10x thinking is a major catalyst for transforming the impact of your organization in your community. If you were to look at the fundraising projects I've had a hand in (which was all of them, because I did the fundraising in the organization I led), you'd note that everything we did was for the long run. We played the long game. It was not an overnight, one-time, one-off situation. If you can run a campaign for 28 years (as we did then), and if you can run a project for 15 years straight (as we did then), what makes that possible? 10x thinking.

We didn't "gear up" at XYZ time of year for XYZ project. It's a way of thinking that drives a way of working that drives an ever-increasing result. We were responsible for it, we were reliable, and our community knew we could be counted on. That's the definition of incredible work. It stands the test of time. Anyone is capable of doing it. Will you?

Thriving Point:

Infuse 10x thinking into everything you do in your organization to fulfill your Mission beyond every expectation.

What is the value of a volunteer in your organization?

I KNEW OF A GENTLEMAN, 65 years old, who had been a volunteer at the local seniors' center for many years. Marvin had been publicly recognized by the mayor for his volunteerism at the center. He decided to volunteer for a local diabetes run/walk, and left home early in his jeans and tennis shoes so he would arrive on time. It wasn't even three hours later that he returned home wearing the light blue t-shirt he received free at the event. The diabetes run/walk wasn't over; in fact, it was an all-day event. When asked about it, Marvin's response was, "Aw, I'm too old for all that."

Whatever may or may not have happened at the diabetes run/walk, it's clear he walked away deflated, and he started to acknowledge within himself and take ownership of something that really wasn't his. If I had to guess, I would say that light blue t-shirt he arrived home in was never worn again.

The value of a t-shirt is that you give it to a participant to extend the life of the feeling after the event. Maybe they'll wear it when they go do something they like, such as a run around the neighbourhood. Maybe they'll wear it to work or to a BBQ. It represents pride for participation and giving. Whatever that shirt represents to the person, it's a sense of belonging. I've gotten t-shirts where just the sight of them took me back to the event and the experience I had there, good or bad. I've had moments of thinking, "I don't want to do that again." If the experience was bad, I put that t-shirt in the bag that went to Goodwill. I moved it out of my world.

If Marvin had gone to the diabetes run/walk and met some new people, and he had been thanked at least once or twice, and had some meaningful role and had been acknowledged, he would've come home and passed out in that t-shirt. The next morning, he would've gotten up and put it on again and gone about his day. People would've said to him, "Hey, were you at that event?" He would've talked about it. And then he would've done laundry and folded his t-shirt. And he probably would've worn it next week.

Instead, I'll bet he either tucked the t-shirt away so he wouldn't see it, or he ended up giving it away. That's because of the people he met at the event and how he felt while he was there. And that is the crux of the issue of volunteerism. Of course there are people who have great memories and who volunteer all their life, but there are also many who get a first taste of volunteering and never return. They just quietly walk away, and they never share their feelings about it to anyone. They don't return for many reasons, but essentially they didn't feel they had a role. I saw it in the organization I led as executive director.

You have to really be on and up and in "sales mode" when you have volunteers, mostly because they just don't know what to do. Sometimes they come in with their ego first. They're gonna run it, take over, push everyone around, and take command. You have to work with that volunteer, too, and bring them down a bit.

As a staff person in an organization that's putting on a race (such as a diabetes run/walk) and passing out the t-shirts, you have to be ready for everyone. Too many volunteers leave without an experience of being valued. What gets missed? It's pretty simple. "I have a need; you're gonna fill it; I don't care about you; I need you to do this now." Plenty of volunteers have exactly that experience. And your staff is the cause.

Volunteers show up to volunteer just as they show up to do everything else. Who you are is who you are when you volunteer. It's usually a quick entry, not much intake, maybe not a lot of time to find out much about you. Let's suppose you go to the Salvation Army and showed up thinking you were gonna go in, take all the clothes and put them on hangers and put them on the racks. But to your surprise, you're in receiving and lifting 50-pound boxes, and you have a bad back. So you limp home the next afternoon. That's a simple example of what happens every day in the volunteer world.

Humans rarely speak up and say, "Hey, I have a bad back," because they want to belong and they want to contribute. So they'll downplay their weak back and **boom**, they're in receiving. We all want to be accepted and fit in. So you're not gonna suddenly throw up your arms and say "I can't do this, I can't do that." You know a staff person is gonna roll their eyes and say, "Then what did you come here for?" In most nonprofits, you're gonna get a volunteer to do whatever crisis presents itself at the time. It's the urgency to get things done without a plan, and volunteers experience the brunt of that.

So as a volunteer, you're going to find yourself over in the corner unpacking boxes. Blake, the guy who directs volunteers, will ask how long you can stay. "Three or four hours," you say. So you stay four hours. When you leave, it's probable that Blake is either gone for the day or he's with another new volunteer. Nobody acknowledges you, thanks you or invites you back as you exit. It seems like a minor point, and it was a bedrock in the organization where I led.

In my organization when I was executive director, every adult and child who left our building was bid "Goodbye, see you later," and "Thanks for coming." In almost every case, they were walked to the door. It's just a human courtesy. That's how we worked. It's not in a textbook somewhere and it's not from a stage. They'll come and give without expectation, but people like to be acknowledged, and that's what they got when they left our building.

Thriving Point:

How you interact with volunteers in your organization tells me how you do everything else in your organization.

What mindset is ruling your nonprofit leadership?

THERE IS AN ORGANIZATION in my community that does a community turkey dinner every year. They probably raise around $10,000. At one point, I heard they decided they didn't think they could do it anymore; it was just too much work, they said. Later I heard they decided that if they continued doing it, they were going to serve roast beef instead of turkey, because of how much time it took to de-bone a turkey.

This is an interesting scenario. Roast beef is a very different approach. If you like red meat, you like red meat. But not everyone does. So where they can get 800 people out to a turkey dinner, they'll get maybe 400 out for roast beef. It would be easier to carve and there would be no bones. But they wouldn't have anywhere near the results.

Instead of listening to the audience, they were listening to the kitchen. Instead of serving what the public wanted or what the following had come to expect, they tweaked a big project they relied on, based on bones and what the kitchen said. Does the event serve the kitchen, or does the event serve the supporters? This is so often how decisions get made at a high level in nonprofits.

How are you approaching what you really want? Are you someone who, if there isn't a barrier there, you're creating one? Because that's what I see playing out every single day. So when you fail, you can say, "See? It didn't work."

You can create whatever you want, and your narrative

will fulfill itself. You have a choice: you can either do a better job, make it amazing and win…or you can keep doing what you do now, and it'll be the same as it's always been, or worse…and you lose. If it's worth doing, do it really well. It comes down to how you operate. Stop setting up yourself and your staff to avoid coping with how things really are.

The energy to win is not common, and losing is everywhere. So right now, it wouldn't surprise me if your default might be to list out all the reasons it won't work, or why you won't win. This mindset permeates executive directors, staff and boards alike. It's easy to be blinded by your reasons and convince yourself that things won't work. It's high time you set out to win…and it begins and ends in your mind.

Thriving Point:

If you want to win in your organization and your leadership, change the narrative from all the reasons you can't into all the reasons you *can*.

How do you handle gossip in a nonprofit organization?

Every organization has it. It's human behaviour, what humans do when they gather. That's the first thing to understand and accept. You will never be rid of it, because it's present whenever groups of humans gather.

As an executive director, you are dealing with 12 marbles all at one time. Most of your staff, however, have one marble, maybe two. That's their focus, so they don't see the other nine or ten marbles. All of a sudden, if there's a bit of anything gossipy or negative or detrimental, they'll have a nice long chew on it; there are always those who are like that. And others will chew quickly, spit it out, and not think about it again.

The trouble begins when there is an appetite for gossip, and it only takes one voice inside your organization to get it started. As executive director, you may hear it. It may come to your attention, and it's like a tripwire. You have to be very careful you don't go in that direction. Your lizard brain might kick in, and you may want to go after it, get it solved, clear it up and deal with it. But that's not always the best route.

We had an incident where one staff was against an idea and the plan, but she wouldn't bring it out. She would chew away on it at the kitchen counter with everyone. She was wailing just out of earshot, but I could tell it was there. I could tell she was the one who planted the seed, and she was watering it every chance she had. There were nine staff at the time, and I adopted a very simple strategy.

We had a massive lobby, so I gathered everyone in the

lobby in a circle. I tossed the issue into the circle and I said, "One of us here has a real problem with this, and one of us here is really taking us down, because one of us here is saying this, this, this and this. And we are all affected. And if this continues, we will all lose." I pointed out what it was doing to the organization, and said, "This is what we're going to have to do from this moment on if we're going to do the work we're here for."

I went around to each one of them and asked, "Is there anything I said that you didn't understand or was unclear?" I asked all nine individually and I was ready for buy-in, consensus, resistance or whatever they were gonna toss at me. Then I went around to the same nine and asked, "Is there something that I should be thinking about that we need to change, or that we need to reconsider?" Again, I asked each one of them. This procedure stopped the issue entirely.

Thriving Point:

Gossip exists in every place where humans gather, and handling it requires bringing a Mission-focused conversation to the table with your staff. What human beings need most is a reminder of the *why*.

How do you deal with chronic indecision inside a nonprofit?

EVERY NONPROFIT faces various levels of indecision. Should we do this fundraising project or not? Should we run this program or not? A multitude of voices will often bring a decision to a grinding halt with no solution in sight. As an executive director, I approached this challenge by asking a simple but powerful question, "What will happen if we *don't* do it?"

I would listen for only so long. I'd attempt to hear everyone's five cents, but there came a point when it was like a train. It gets so long that it doesn't remember what station it left. Whenever I used this question, it was like the gavel hit the table. I inserted it very abruptly. "What will happen if we *don't* do it?" That question inevitably halted everyone and sidetracked everything they said without getting to a solution or a decision, and it caused them to shift their thinking.

There is a danger when you get into group thinking. Everyone has their opinion why it won't work and why it should be delayed. But when you ask this question, now they have to say something totally different than what's been rambling in their head. It also brings them back to the *why* of the Mission. They have to start looking at it and saying, "Well, there would be no XYZ program." *Exactly!* And that is why we must find the how-to, we must find the money, and we must find the people to make this happen. Because the Mission demands it.

For clarity, you don't open a conversation with this question, nor do you insert it early in a meeting. You certainly play this card when the momentum is building against an idea or going off in the wrong direction. I use it very strategically for that purpose.

Let's say the activity or event you're deciding on is going to have a high price tag. Perhaps you're trying to decide whether or not to put on an addition to a homeless shelter. You don't know if you should add those other 40 beds because, well, what if you can't get the money? Space, money, timeline—all those things are real and valid. But what will happen if you don't open those 40 beds?

Now you have to start thinking like the user. Now you can start thinking of what happens if we don't, which shifts the thinking to, "Wow, we should find this money, we should get these partners. And let's start sketching out how it's going to happen."

This question can be posed in an even simpler scenario. It could be something mundane in your workday. For example, reminding a staff member to be sure to get a particular post out on Facebook or another channel. The staff says, "Oh, I'll do it tomorrow or the next day." What if you don't tell the world about it today though? So many things get delayed because people like to control their own timeline. They like to delay the work until later. But what if you don't do it now? Who doesn't hear about it?

The most common place this comes up in a nonprofit is a *thank you*. People in organizations are notorious for not saying thank you enough, or in a timely manner. It always comes at the bottom of the list or the end of the workload. This is where organizations trip up every day. They forget to ask, "What will happen if we don't thank our donors?" The answer, of course, is obvious: they will go somewhere else.

Want another everyday example? You're interviewing three people for a position. One is just top notch — your first choice, the one person you most want to hire. And there are two other people on the hiring committee, and they say, "Oh, well maybe we should wait and go back through the résumés." But what happens if we don't hire Jared? What happens if there's nobody else on the list? Jared has all these qualifications. The answer is that he gets hired somewhere else and takes his skills there. It's like bringing a board member on mid-term. Most organizations say, "Oh yes, we have a vacancy. Well we know that Peter's resigned or left. We'll wait until the annual meeting next year."

What if you **don't** wait until the annual meeting? What if you look out into the community now and say, "Who is best to come in and take that spot?" But no, everybody just defers to the future when there's a date on the calendar that gives them a reason to do it. What will happen if you wait is that you'll have an empty seat and a missed opportunity. Every single time.

Thriving Point:

Moving the Mission forward faster means asking what will happen if you **don't** do it.

How do you ensure this year will be different from last in your organization?

L ET'S ASK THIS QUESTION in a real way. If you have a disaster, how do you turn it around? Where do you start? This a great question, particularly because most nonprofits are disasters on some level. Acknowledged or unacknowledged, it's a reality, and very simply, you need to raise your level of give a damn. Here's a starting point.

If you can recognize your board is a problem, or your staff is a problem, or fundraising is a problem…if you can name the problem, you own the responsibility to change it. Can you walk away and not look back? Yes, of course. Many executive directors do this, as evidenced by the average tenure of executive directors in the sector. Trouble is, you're going to walk out of one situation straight into another…and you'll just keep doing what you've always done. The same disaster you face where you are now will show up in every organization you choose to lead.

It's easy to expect others to clean up the mess. Ask yourself, what switch did you turn off within yourself when you could see it and name it, but then didn't take the time to change it? You weren't born to sit and watch. If you were, you would not be in the nonprofit sector.

I have always tended to notice things. On one occasion, I noticed the floor mats needed to be cleaned. Did I walk through purposely to see the mats? No, but I was always aware of what is right and what needed to be righted, and on that visit, it was the mats. I knew I had some staff who swiveled their heads and said, "How does she even see those mats when this, that and the other thing are crushing us right now?"

It's a way of being to have your finger on the button that makes change. You have to constantly be watching for everything. Once you're willing, aware, open and observing, it's very easy to notice everything. It's when you decide to ignore, look the other way, or not do something that you start to slide down a hill. Suddenly you're saying, "There's nothing I can do about it." You've gone so far down that the effort seems too great and the timing seems too late. Once you accept that, it becomes your reality. It's what you'll be known for, and you won't reach the people who could make the change for you.

When you don't encourage the people in your organization to be problem solvers it's like a cancer. Everything you see is a chance to make a choice, and if you choose indecision, you end up with a disaster. That's a choice you make every day. Indecision creates disasters faster than anything else.

Thriving Point:

The prerequisite to turning around any circumstance in your organization is to first identify when and where you stopped noticing. Flip the switch within yourself.

How do you create magic in your organization?

WHAT IS THE MOST MAGICAL THING that could happen to you and your organization? Most fundraisers and people in the nonprofit sector would say, "If somebody came in and dropped a bucket of money on us." Your version of magic would likely hinge on the dollar symbol.

I have a very different viewpoint. The most magic I've experienced is all the people with whom I cross paths. Their gender and age don't matter. Every one of them gets filed away in my brain as to what they have a passion for that can make something easier and quicker, or can provide a solution. I look and listen to see what their strengths are and what they do really well. Money might come later, and it rarely comes first. People are carrying around a wealth of information inside their head that hasn't come out. In fact, I often find in a very quick conversation that what they love to do and what they're good at hasn't come out in two decades.

If you're looking at your whole organization, there are important pieces of work that can be farmed out, passed on, or offered to someone who probably has never been a donor. They haven't even given ten dollars, yet they could do something that is immensely valuable to you. Does it sometimes *not* include dollars through the door and into the coffers? Yes. Does that mean they have no value? Absolutely not.

Of course money is the thing you want, and you have the capacity to create money with the magic you find in people. In the organization I led, there is a huge retention rate of people who have been involved and stay involved. All it required was igniting what they already said they love to do. To this day, I have a fluid inventory of people and what they like to do. And when I get with them, I know that together we are going to do the best work possible.

When you need information technology support, you call an IT company, right? But I didn't necessarily do that. Instead, I remembered talking to Glen who was a truck driver. Fourteen years ago, we got into a conversation, and I discovered he did all kinds of IT work on the side because he was passionate about it, and good at it. From trucking to technology, he was self-taught. He lived his passion. So when I needed IT work, Glen was the first person I called. Years later, Glen is still doing the IT work for that organization.

Every person has a passion for something. Your job is to uncover it. And when you want something done well, done right, and done on time, go to that person. I maintain a fluid mental inventory of people, and it comes from careful listening. I regularly swing back to people I crossed paths with months and years ago.

Thriving Point:

The "magic" you seek isn't a bucket of money. Rather, it's found when you adopt the attitude that everyone you meet matters. You have no idea who has magic in them that will take your organization and your Mission to the next level.

In Closing

"What have I learned?"

To begin, the model of work is the creation of someone. The model could be 9 to 5 Monday through Friday, or a work "shift", or even a four-day work week. Regardless, most work models are someone else's template we consume because we don't create our own. Work is where you spend at least 1/3 of your life. That's a lot of days to get up and look in the mirror.

I've always seen to it that my work has purpose and meaning — and a bit of knowing, that just by being in the presence of someone, they had a better life or a better chance. People pursue wealth and it doesn't change their heart. I've been told many times, "You could've done so much better in the private sector". I'm sure that is true, financially speaking. And that was never my goal.

When I used to go to *Favourites* in my phone, the first entry was office/work. Anyone who truly knows me would not be surprised by that. However, I know now, that office/work doesn't belong in the first entry of my *Favourites*. That is one thing I've learned. Now that I am making my own way, my work has changed. I no longer have a number to dial into. These days, I dial into me.

We all know Steve Jobs, and most of us have heard the address he gave at the Stanford University Convocation in

2005. Have you ever gone back to look at his last words when he was sick in the hospital? I try to read it every January as a stark reminder: *"I have looked in the mirror every morning and asked myself: If today were the last day of my life, would I want to do what I am about to do today?"*

The work I chose in the non-profit sector has given me the most satisfaction. It has given me more memories of people I would never have met if I had not chosen to do this work. In my executive director career, I worked with 526 board members. That's a lot of people to strive to get to know and understand. Then I think of the staff and volunteers. Add to that the 800 people who came to fundraising events every year. I knew them all by name. And then add 30,000 Gold Rush players. I have a vault full of people, many of whom I've known superficially or casually. But many I know quite well. Above all, I know what is important to them.

Would I recommend the non-profit sector as a career? Maybe. It's a tough go. If the non-profit sector had a symbolic tree, it would be the weeping willow — which is rooted in hope, a sense of belonging, and safety. The roots of a weeping willow are shallow. A strong wind would cause it to topple over. Sadly, that's the story of too many nonprofits. A good cause that is much needed is trying to make its way forward with no resources, no stability, and a chronic balance sheet of deficits. A storm of any kind — such as a funding shortfall, the loss of key staff, or board chaos — can bring important work to a halt. Far too many non-profits live on the precarious edge of closure.

What I've learned is that in order to do non-profit work well, you need a bucket load of patience. You need to listen more than you talk. And you need to play the long game. There are no shortcuts to doing great work. I rewrote the typical non-profit narrative by playing the long game. It was how I showed up every day that made the difference. I left my ego at home and brought my purpose instead. I tapped into the talent of others. And I would do it all again!

There are things in my career that I wish I had learned sooner. But that's a life cycle. You can only learn them as you do them. "If I had only known that then"—well, that's not how a compass works. That's a map. If you want to have guidelines and someone else to create your path, use a map. If you want to create your own path, use a compass. Figure it out. If you get lost, try again. People who rely on GPS are hilarious to me. It's like your own phone—if everyone you know is recorded by name, you don't know their phone number. GPS does the same thing. You no longer know buildings, landmarks, north, or south. It does your thinking for you. That was never the career I wanted. I chart my own path.

Looking back, I would take more vacation. I would be more content with okay than getting it perfectly right. For too many years, I wanted to do it the best possible. I didn't understand that okay is good. Now I know to get things out there, and much sooner. That is a critical learning.

"Remembering that you are going to die is the best way I know to avoid the trap of thinking you have something to lose. You are already naked. There is no reason not to follow your heart."

— Steve Jobs

About the Author

Sheree Allison's career as an executive director spans 30 years for only one organization, which is Big Brothers Big Sisters and Boys & Girls Clubs of Miramichi, New Brunswick, Canada.

Sheree, her work and her accomplishments are widely known, but she never talks of her success. Only her colleagues speak of the magnitude and scope of what she accomplished and what it took to get there. Her results are remarkable considering her humble beginnings. Sheree started her working life as a teacher. Though she enjoyed it, she wanted more than bells ringing. She knew early on that she wanted to take risks and break molds.

When Sheree stumbled into a job in a non-profit, she had no idea what she was getting into. Until that moment, a "board" in her mind was a 2x4. What Sheree attempted to do in a small community on a shoestring budget is unheard of. She had very little support but that didn't deter her. The ultimate triumph wasn't luck, rather it was hard work and a lot of skills driving it. Through it all, Sheree was never swayed from the mission by popularity, validation, manipulation, coercion, or force.

In terms of results achieved — the revenue streams of Big Brothers Big Sisters/Boys & Girls Club of Miramichi went from $250,000 in year 2000 to $3,200,000 in year 2020. The organization's annual budget is $1.3 million raised in a community of 25,000 people. Big

Brothers Big Sisters/Boys & Girls Club of Miramichi is the #1 provider and facilitator of mentoring programs, after school programs and summer camps in the greater community. In addition, they are the sole provider of the School Breakfast Program that serves 5139 kids in 23 schools. Most notably, Sheree and the board established a foundation with the goal of a 10-year financial investment. After three years, they surpassed 40% to goal.

Proud to call herself 100% responsible for raising the money in her organization, Sheree is indeed the chief fundraiser. When she gets an idea, she acts on it. Where most people have their heads down, Sheree's eyes are scanning the landscape looking for what's working. Where most people wallow in their mistakes, Sheree moves right on. And her most valuable skill is patience in abundance. She gave her all to birthing a dream, and it worked!

As an executive director, Sheree has worked from one end of the spectrum (nowhere near enough money in the budget to hire enough staff and pay all the bills) to the opposite end of the spectrum (more money coming in than they knew what to do with) and the scrutiny and criticism that accompanies it. She experienced both and made it out on the other side.

The boardroom is where Sheree shines — not because of ego or the need for attention — but because she knows what to provide that moves decisions forward. She is a marketing innovator and expert, and a human resources expert by default. Despite making loads of mistakes, she managed to build a world-class organization with amazing staff who love the mission and their work.

As of this writing, "author" is the cherry that tops a list of extraordinary accomplishments, and most importantly, a career and life filled with joy and purpose.